NOW AVAILABLE

The programs described in this book are now available on disk for your IBM PC (and most compatibles). They have been written in C and you will need to have a C compiler. (The author used Lattice C$^{(TM)}$.) Your computer will also need an IBM graphics adaptor or Hercules$^{(TM)}$ graphics board.

Order the Program Disk today priced **£9.78 including VAT/$14.95** from your computer store, bookseller or by using the order form below.

Ammeraal: **Programming Principles in Computer Graphics** – Program Disk

Please send me .... copies of the Ammeraal: Programming Principles in Computer Graphics – Program Disk at **£9.78 including VAT/$14.95** each

IBM PC   0 471 91271 9

POSTAGE AND HANDLING FREE FOR CASH WITH ORDER OF PAYMENT BY CREDIT CARD

☐ Remittance enclosed .... Allow approx. 14 days for delivery
☐ Please charge this order to my credit card (All orders subject to credit approval)
Delete as necessary:—AMERICAN EXPRESS, DINERS CLUB, BARCLAYCARD/VISA, ACCESS

CARD NUMBER [| | | | | | | | | | | | | | | | |] Expiration date ....
☐ Please send me an invoice for prepayment. A small postage and handling charge will be made.
Software purchased for professional purposes is generally recognized as tax deductible.
☐ Please keep me informed of new books in my subject area which is ....

NAME/ADDRESS ....
....
....
OFFICIAL ORDER No .... SIGNATURE ....

If you have any queries about the compatability of your hardware configuration, please contact:

Helen Ramsey
John Wiley & Sons Limited
Baffins Lane
Chichester
West Sussex
PO19 1UD
England

Customer Service Department
John Wiley & Sons Limited
Shripney Road
Bognor Regis
West Sussex
PO22 9SA

Programming Principles
in Computer Graphics

Programming Principles in Computer Graphics

L. Ammeraal

Christelijke Hogere Technische School
Hilversum, The Netherlands

JOHN WILEY & SONS
Chichester · New York · Brisbane · Toronto · Singapore

Copyright © 1986 by John Wiley & Sons Ltd.

Reprinted with corrections February 1987

Library of Congress Cataloging-in-Publication Data:

Ammeraal, L.
  Programming principles in computer graphics.

  Bibliography: p.
  Includes index
1. Electronic digital computers—Programming.
2. Computer graphics.   I. Title.
QA76.6.A466   1986   006.6′6   85-29590
ISBN 0 471 90989 0

British Library Cataloging in Publication Data:

Ammeraal, L.
  Programming principles in computer graphics.
  1. Computer graphics   2. Electronic digital
  computers—Programming
  I. Title
  006.6′6   T385

ISBN 0 471 90989 0

Printed and bound in Great Britain.

Contents

v

Preface

This book deals with the most essential elements of computer graphics, namely analytic geometry and programming. It explains how programmers can use plotters and other graphics devices without discussing in detail how these devices work, and in what types they are now available. I hope that the reader will appreciate such a device-independent approach. In any case we thus avoid the confusion that sometimes arises if hardware and software topics are intertwined.

Much attention is paid to the graphical representation of three-dimensional objects. The first three chapters contain a few interesting programs such as one for B-spline curve fitting, but these chapters are also preparatory for the rest of the book. Chapter 4 gives the traditional transformations for wire-frame models. In contrast to this well-known subject, Chapter 5 introduces an efficient method for hidden-line elimination which, as far as I know, is new. Like all other algorithms in the book, the method is worked out in a complete program, called *HIDLINPIX*. Some applications of this program are given in Chapter 6. Since some of the programs may well be useful in practice, the book offers more than the 'principles' promised in its title. On the other hand, there are also some programs of a somewhat playful nature, which have no practical significance in themselves. I hope that in these programs the reader will find principles that also apply to more realistic problems.

All programs in the book are expressed in the C language. This might seem curious, since Pascal is more frequently used for such purposes. Having programmed in a great many languages for more than a quarter of a century I would rate Pascal as very good but C as excellent. (Since I have written successful Dutch textbooks for them, I wish a long life to both languages!) It is difficult to prove that braces { } are at least as readable as the keywords *begin* or *end,* but the difference in length is obvious. I mention this because for some programs in this book only the compactness of the C language made it feasible to list them completely.

Up to now I have delayed answering the difficult question for whom the book is intended. I do not know the curricula of universities and other institutions all over the world well enough to recommend the book for term X in course Y. However, it seems that for anyone who teaches computer graphics, at least some parts of the book will be useful. For example, simple solid objects can be drawn in perspective by preparing an input file for *HIDLINPIX* manually, so that even those readers who do not program could benefit from the book. There are exercises at the end of each chapter but I am convinced that any teacher in this field can easily add problems to his or her personal taste.

In the professional world many people are developing software packages for computer aided design. I hope that the book will also be useful in this area, and that it will be a modest contribution to the development of good products.

L. Ammeraal

CHAPTER 1

Introduction

1.1 A MOTIVATION FOR GRAPHICS PROGRAMMING

Students will sometimes doubt the relevance of the things they have to learn and they will ask their teachers questions about them. If little time is available, a brief but unsatisfactory answer to such questions will simply consist of a reference to the examination requiring that knowledge. Fortunately, it is most unlikely for such questions to be asked if the subject matter is related to computer graphics. Compared with the usual listings of a line printer, graphics computer output is very attractive to look at, and even those who do not agree with this are convinced that computer graphics has useful applications.

Far more satisfying than looking at graphics computer output is producing such results oneself. This do-it-yourself point of view applies to all arts, but in computer graphics we are in the unique position of having an extremely accurate and hard-working slave at our disposal. This slave can produce literally all kinds of drawn pictures, unless we are unable to instruct it how to do it. Unfortunately, the latter is not an exception but a rule. Most computer users are unable to make the computer draw the pictures they want, even if they spend a lot of money on software. We have to live with this unsatisfactory situation because it is impossible for the average computer-user to write all the software he needs. We have to buy software written by others. This does not imply that it should be unwise to train students in programming. We should remember that before software is available it must be written. It is highly improbable that all the software we need will soon be available, so in future, programming will be necessary. This applies particularly to graphics software, since many programs that produce tables will be replaced with those which have graphics output.

Even those users who do not program but buy all the software they need will benefit from some knowledge of programming. Students should deal with concepts that will not be quickly outdated but will be valid forever. An algorithm to decide whether or not a surface in space hides a line segment is such a fundamental concept, whereas technical details of a commercially available program package are not. Of course, sooner or later the users of such a package have to study its details thoroughly, but by then they should already have some insight into graphics algorithms. Such insight is best acquired by studying the algorithms both theoretically and practically. It is therefore recommended to program yourself, even if you think you will not be programming in the future.

1.2 GRAPHICS PROGRAMMING AND THE C LANGUAGE

Natural languages, though interesting in many respects, are inadequate to express algorithms. Not surprisingly, algorithms are best written in an algorithmic language.

1

An algorithmic language which is 'understood' by computers is called a high-level programming language, or, briefly, a programming language. We shall conform to this usage, but stipulate that the programming language be truly 'high-level': not only machines but also human beings should understand the language as efficiently and as easily as possible. We do not ask that the language be easily readable for everyone. Mathematical symbols are unreadable for most eight-year-old children but are almost indispensable for mathematicians and engineers. In much the same way the programming language we shall use will not be appreciated by everyone, but it has proved to be extremely useful for professional programmers. We shall use the C language, not only because it is widespread but also because of the qualities of the language itself. To program in C one must be accurate; in C, logical errors will lead to syntactic errors less often than in Pascal, for example. Such logical errors in a C program may lead to wrong results or messages with technical errors that are hard to understand. In other words, mistakes could have bad effects. We have to realize this if we write C programs. If we read them we want our programs to be easily readable, which is a completely different aspect. People who do not use this language themselves will sometimes think C programs too cryptic to be readable. A good deal of confusion exists about readability. If one line of a C program corresponds to ten lines of Basic it is unfair to complain that a single line of C text is not as readable as one of those ten lines in Basic. If we try to understand a short C program and presume that it must be simple because it is short, we shall be disappointed. This should be remembered on many occasions in this book; a very short C program might be non-trivial and even interesting!

For a systematic study of C, some books on this language are mentioned in the Bibliography. As to explaining remarks on the C language, we shall restrict ourselves to notations that are very specific for it. More facts about the C language can be found in the Appendix. Here is our first graphics C program:

```
/* SQUARES: This program draws 50 squares inside each other */
main()
{ float xA, yA, xB, yB, xC, yC, xD, yD,
    xxA, yyA, xxB, yyB, xxC, yyC, xxD, yyD, p, q;
  int i;
  p=0.95; q=1.0-p;
  xA=2.0; xB=8.0; xC=8.0; xD=2.0;
  yA=0.5; yB=0.5; yC=6.5; yD=6.5;
  initgr();
  for (i=0; i<50; i++)
  { move(xA, yA);
    draw(xB, yB); draw(xC, yC); draw(xD, yD); draw(xA, yA);
    xxA=p*xA+q*xB; yyA=p*yA+q*yB; xxB=p*xB+q*xC; yyB=p*yB+q*yC;
    xxC=p*xC+q*xD; yyC=p*yC+q*yD; xxD=p*xD+q*xA; yyD=p*yD+q*yA;
    xA=xxA; xB=xxB; xC=xxC; xD=xxD;
    yA=yyA; yB=yyB; yC=yyC; yD=yyD;
  }
  endgr();
}
```

The output of this program is shown in Fig. 1.1.

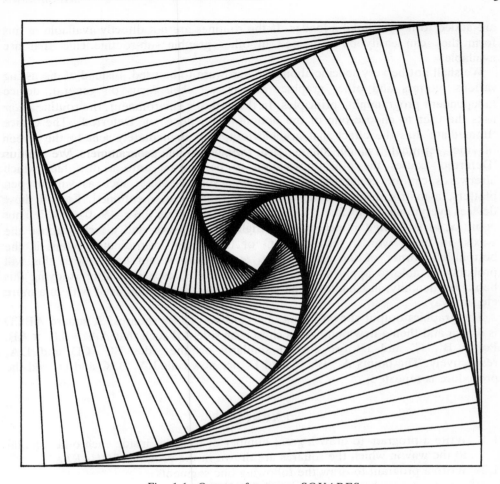

Fig. 1.1. Output of program SQUARES

The program contains calls of four graphic routines:

initgr( )   initializes graphic output;
move(x, y)   moves a (real or fictitious) pen to point (x, y);
draw(x, y)   draws a line segment from the current position of the pen to point
            (x, y);
endgr( )   performs final actions such as clearing an output buffer.

In C the technical term for 'procedure' or '(sub)routine' is 'function'. Function calls are written with parentheses, even if there are no arguments. The call *initgr*( ) is required before the functions *move* and *draw* can be called. Similarly, the final call of *move* or *draw* must be followed by a call of *endgr*. Both calls *move*(x, y) and *draw*(x, y) move a (real or fictitious) pen to point (x, y); with *move*(x, y) the pen is up and with *draw*(x, y) it is down. The four functions mentioned do not belong to the C language. They are external routines; after compilation of our program they are added to it by a linking loader. If the routines are not directly available in this form they can easily be expressed in other graphic sub-routine calls that are available.

We shall not be very specific about the hardware to be used. Instead of discussing various plotters and other graphics devices we shall focus on general, device independent programming principles. In the author's environment, the routine *initgr* asks the user to choose one of the options 'Immediate' or 'Deferred'. The choice 'Immediate' has the effect that graphics output is immediately sent to the screen of the terminal, which offers the possibility of interaction. The option 'Deferred' causes the plot information to be written onto a disk file, which afterwards can be converted and sent to several devices, such as various pen plotters, a matrix printer or the graphics terminal just mentioned. For all these devices everything works fine if the ranges for x and y are $0 \leqslant x \leqslant 9$, $0 \leqslant y \leqslant 7$. Thus point (x, y) is located x inches to the right of the y-axis and y inches above the x-axis, in other words, the origin O of the screen co-ordinate system is the bottom-left corner of the screen. The reader who is not happy with this will probably be able to apply a change of co-ordinates, especially after studying this book! Incidentally, in Chapter 2 the picture boundaries will be dealt with in a more elegant way.

The graphics output shown in Fig. 1.1 consists of fifty squares. A square ABCD is drawn and then a new point A′ is chosen on side AB such that $AA' = 0.05 \times AB$. Points B′, C′ and D′ are chosen similarly on the sides BC, CD and DA, respectively. The points A′, B′, C′ and D′ are now called A, B, C and D, and the procedure is repeated.

EXERCISES

1.1 Write a program to draw a great number of triangles inside each other similar to the way in which the squares are drawn in the program *SQUARES*.

1.2 Write a program to draw the following line segments:

From point $(1.0, 6.0)$ to point $(1.0, 1.0)$;
From point $(1.0, 5.8)$ to point $(1.2, 1.0)$;
From point $(1.0, 5.6)$ to point $(1.4, 1.0)$;

· · ·

From point $(1.0, 1.0)$ to point $(6.0, 1.0)$.

CHAPTER 2

Two-dimensional algorithms

2.1 TRANSFORMATIONS AND NEW CO-ORDINATES

Consider the following system of equations

$$\begin{cases} x' = x + a \\ y' = y \end{cases}$$

We can interpret these equations in two ways:

(1) All points in the xy-plane move a distance a to the right (see Fig. 2.1(a)).
(2) The x- and y-axes move a distance a to the left (see Fig. 2.1(b)).

This simple example shows a principle which also applies to more complex situations. We shall often deal with systems of equations, usually written as matrix products, and interpret them as a transformation of all points in a fixed co-ordinate system. However, the same system of equations can then be interpreted as a change of co-ordinates.

We wish to rotate point $P(x, y)$ through an angle φ about the origin O. The image point will be called $P'(x', y')$ (see Fig. 2.2). Then there are numbers a, b, c, d such that x' and y' can be derived from x and y as follows:

$$\begin{cases} x' = ax + by \\ y' = cx + dy \end{cases} \tag{2.1}$$

The values of a, b, c, d can be obtained by choosing first $(x, y) = (1, 0)$. Setting $x = 1$ and $y = 0$ in Eq. (2.1) we get:

$$x' = a$$
$$y' = c$$

However, in this simple case the values of x' and y' are $\cos \varphi$ and $\sin \varphi$, as can be seen in Fig. 2.3(a). Thus we have:

$$a = \cos \varphi$$
$$c = \sin \varphi$$

In the same way, Fig. 2.3(b) leads to:

$$b = -\sin \varphi$$
$$d = \cos \varphi$$

Thus for Eqs (2.1) we now write:

$$\begin{cases} x' = x \cos \varphi - y \sin \varphi \\ y' = x \sin \varphi + y \cos \varphi \end{cases} \tag{2.2}$$

5

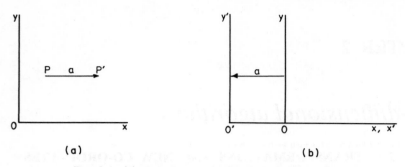

Fig. 2.1. (a) *Translation*; (b) *change of co-ordinates*

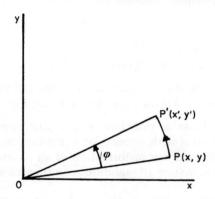

Fig. 2.2. *Rotation about O through angle* φ

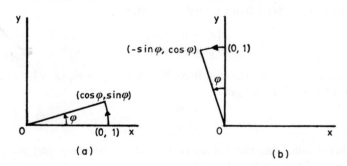

Fig. 2.3. (a) *Image of* $(1, 0)$; (b) *image of* $(0, 1)$

In the following program an arrow is rotated repeatedly through 6° about O and then drawn.

```
/* QUADRANT1:                                                     */
/* This program draws 14 arrows, flying counter-clockwise         */
/* about O in the first quadrant of the coordinate system         */

#include <math.h>
float x[4]={ 6.0,    6.0,    5.9,    6.1}, /*  See Figure below    */
      y[4]={-0.25,  0.25,   0.0,    0.0}; /*  in this program     */
```

```
main()
{ int i,  j;
  float pi, phi, cos_phi, sin_phi, xx, yy;
  pi=4.0*atan(1.0);  phi=6*pi/180;
  cos_phi=cos(phi);  sin_phi=sin(phi);
  initgr();
  for (i=1; i<=14; i++)                  /*  Initial position  */
  { /*  Rotate the arrow: */             /*   of the arrow:    */
    for (j=0; j<=3; j++)                  /*                    */
    { xx=x[j]; yy=y[j];                   /*      (6, 0.25)     */
      x[j]=xx*cos_phi-yy*sin_phi;         /*         1          */
      y[j]=xx*sin_phi+yy*cos_phi;         /*         ^          */
    }                                     /*        /!\         */
    /*  Draw the rotated arrow: */        /*       2/___\3      */
    move(x[0], y[0]);                     /* (5.9, 0)! (6.1, 0) */
    for (j=1; j<=3; j++)                  /*         !          */
        draw(x[j], y[j]);                 /*         0          */
    draw(x[1], y[1]);                     /*      (6, -0.25)    */
  }
  endgr();
}
```

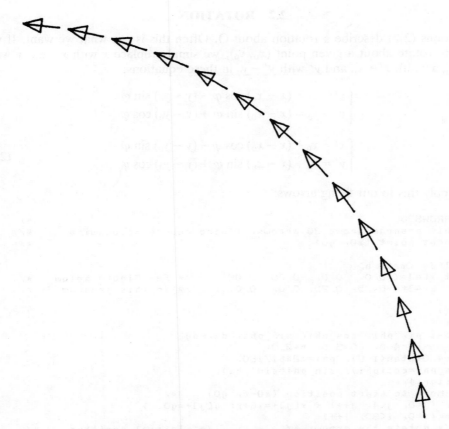

Fig. 2.4. Output of program QUADRANT1

In geometry points of an object are usually denoted by letters A, B, . . . Instead we use integers $0, 1, \ldots$ here. In the initial position the arrow points upwards; its centre is then located in $(6, 0)$. In the right-hand side of the program a not-too-successful attempt has been made to show the arrow in this position. The x- and y-co-ordinates of the *i*th vertex of an arrow are stored in the array elements $x[i]$ and $y[i]$ ($i = 0, 1, 2, 3$). The arrays x and y are external: their definition is outside the function *main*. External arrays have the pleasing property that they can be initialized. Array subscripts count from 0 and we specify the number of elements. Hence the definition (also called declaration)

$$\textit{float } x[4] = \{6.0, 6.0, 5.9, 6.1\}, \ldots$$

introduces four array elements with their initial values:

$$x[0] = 6.0 \qquad x[1] = 6.0 \qquad x[2] = 5.9 \qquad x[3] = 6.1$$

Although initially $y[0]$ is negative and all co-ordinates to be plotted must be positive, there is no problem, since, before the arrow is drawn, it is rotated, which brings it above the x-axis. Figure 2.4 shows the output of this program.

2.2 ROTATION

Equations (2.2) describe a rotation about O. Often this is not what we want. If we wish to rotate about a given point (x_0, y_0), we simply replace x with $x - x_0$, y with $y - y_0$, x' with $x' - x_0$ and y' with $y' - y_0$ in these equations:

$$\begin{cases} x' - x_0 = (x - x_0) \cos \varphi - (y - y_0) \sin \varphi \\ y' - y_0 = (x - x_0) \sin \varphi + (y - y_0) \cos \varphi \end{cases}$$

$$\begin{cases} x' = x_0 + (x - x_0) \cos \varphi - (y - y_0) \sin \varphi \\ y' = y_0 + (x - x_0) \sin \varphi + (y - y_0) \cos \varphi \end{cases} \tag{2.3}$$

We apply this to our flying arrows:

```
/* ARROWS30:                                                      */
/* This program draws 30 arrows, flying counter-clockwise         */
/* about point (x0, y0)                                           */

#include <math.h>
float x[4]={ 0.0,    0.0,  -0.08,  0.08},    /* See Figure below  */
      y[4]={-0.25,   0.25,  0.0,   0.0 };    /* in this program   */

main()
{ int i, j;
  float pi, phi, cos_phi, sin_phi, dx, dy,
        x0=4.5, y0=3.5, r=3.0;
  pi=4.0*atan(1.0); phi=12*pi/180;
  cos_phi=cos(phi); sin_phi=sin(phi);
  initgr();
  /* Move to start position (x0+r, y0) :   */
  for (j=0; j<4; j++) { x[j]+=x0+r; y[j]+=y0; }
  for (i=0; i<30; i++)
  { /* Rotate the arrow: */              /*  Initial position:  */
    for (j=0; j<4; j++)                  /*                     */
```

```
{ dx=x[j]-x0; dy=y[j]-y0;           /*            (0, 0.25)   */
  x[j]=x0+dx*cos_phi-dy*sin_phi;    /*                1       */
  y[j]=y0+dx*sin_phi+dy*cos_phi;    /*                ^       */
}                                   /*               /!\      */
/* Draw the rotated arrow: */       /*             2/_|_\3    */
move(x[0], y[0]);                   /*(-0.08, 0)  |  (0.08, 0)*/
for (j=1; j<=3; j++)                /*                |       */
        draw(x[j], y[j]);           /*                |       */
draw(x[1], y[1]);                   /*                0       */
}                                   /*            (0, -0.25)  */
endgr();
}
```

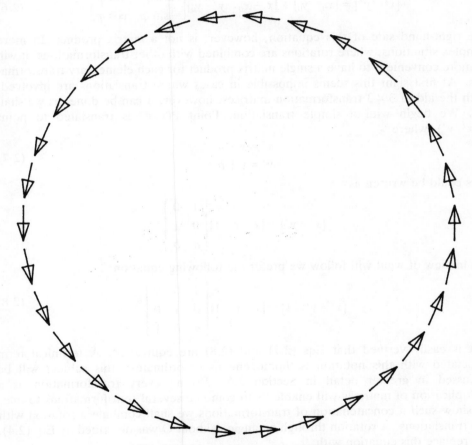

Fig. 2.5. Output of program ARROWS30

Figure 2.5 shows the output of this program.

2.3 MATRIX NOTATION

Equations (2.2) can be written as one matrix equation:

$$[x' \quad y'] = [x \quad y]\begin{bmatrix} \cos\varphi & \sin\varphi \\ -\sin\varphi & \cos\varphi \end{bmatrix} \tag{2.4}$$

or, with column vectors:

$$\begin{bmatrix} x' \\ y' \end{bmatrix} = \begin{bmatrix} \cos\varphi & -\sin\varphi \\ \sin\varphi & \cos\varphi \end{bmatrix} \begin{bmatrix} x \\ y \end{bmatrix} \tag{2.5}$$

In books on computer graphics the row vector notation (2.4) is more frequently used than the column vector notation (2.5). We too shall use notation (2.4). In this notation the ith row of the square matrix is always the image of the ith unit vector (here $i = 1, 2$). It is possible to express Eqs (2.3) as a matrix equation:

$$[x' \quad y'] = [x_0 \quad y_0] + [x - x_0 \quad y - y_0] \begin{bmatrix} \cos\varphi & \sin\varphi \\ -\sin\varphi & \cos\varphi \end{bmatrix} \tag{2.6}$$

The right-hand side of this equation, however, is not a matrix product. In more complex situations, where rotations are combined with other transformations, it will be more convenient to have a single matrix product for each elementary transformation. At first sight this seems impossible in cases where translations are involved. With the aid of 3×3 transformation matrices, however, it can be done, as we shall see. We begin with a simple translation. Point $P(x, y)$ is translated to point $P'(x', y')$, where

$$\begin{aligned} x' &= x + a \\ y' &= y + b \end{aligned} \tag{2.7}$$

This could be written as

$$[x' \quad y'] = [x \quad y \quad 1] \begin{bmatrix} 1 & 0 \\ 0 & 1 \\ a & b \end{bmatrix}$$

but in view of what will follow we prefer the following equation:

$$[x' \quad y' \quad 1] = [x \quad y \quad 1] \begin{bmatrix} 1 & 0 & 0 \\ 0 & 1 & 0 \\ a & b & 1 \end{bmatrix} \tag{2.8}$$

It is easily verified that Eqs (2.7) and (2.8) are equivalent. A technical term associated with this notation is 'homogeneous co-ordinates'; this subject will be discussed in greater detail in Section 3.6. Writing every transformation as a multiplication of matrices will enable us to combine several transformations to one. To show such a concatenation of transformations we shall combine a rotation with two translations. A rotation through an angle φ about O was described by Eq. (2.4). We replace this equation with:

$$[x' \quad y' \quad 1] = [x \quad y \quad 1] \begin{bmatrix} \cos\varphi & \sin\varphi & 0 \\ -\sin\varphi & \cos\varphi & 0 \\ 0 & 0 & 1 \end{bmatrix} \tag{2.9}$$

We shall now derive a new version of Eq. (2.6) to describe a rotation about (x_0, y_0) through an angle φ; this equation will be of the form

$$[x' \quad y' \quad 1] = [x \quad y \quad 1]R \tag{2.10}$$

where R is a 3×3 matrix. To find this matrix R we look upon the transformation as a succession of the following three steps with (u_1, v_1) and (u_2, v_2) as intermediate points:

(1) A translation to move (x_0, y_0) to O:

$$[u_1 \quad v_1 \quad 1] = [x \quad y \quad 1]T'$$

where

$$T' = \begin{bmatrix} 1 & 0 & 0 \\ 0 & 1 & 0 \\ -x_0 & -y_0 & 1 \end{bmatrix}$$

(2) A rotation through angle φ about O:

$$[u_2 \quad v_2 \quad 1] = [u_1 \quad v_1 \quad 1]R_0$$

where

$$R_0 = \begin{bmatrix} \cos \varphi & \sin \varphi & 0 \\ -\sin \varphi & \cos \varphi & 0 \\ 0 & 0 & 1 \end{bmatrix} \qquad (2.11)$$

(3) A translation from O to (x_0, y_0):

$$[x' \quad y' \quad 1] = [u_2 \quad v_2 \quad 1]T$$

where

$$T = \begin{bmatrix} 1 & 0 & 0 \\ 0 & 1 & 0 \\ x_0 & y_0 & 1 \end{bmatrix}$$

The combination of these three steps is based on the fact that matrix multiplication is associative, that is,

$$(AB)C = A(BC)$$

for any three matrices A, B and C whose dimensions are such that these multiplications are possible. For either side of this equation we simply write ABC.

We now find:

$$\begin{aligned}
[x' \quad y' \quad 1] &= [u_2 \quad v_2 \quad 1]T \\
&= \{[u_1 \quad v_1 \quad 1]R_0\}T \\
&= [u_1 \quad v_1 \quad 1]R_0 T \\
&= \{[x \quad y \quad 1]T'\}R_0 T \\
&= [x \quad y \quad 1]T'R_0 T \\
&= [x \quad y \quad 1]R
\end{aligned}$$

where

$$R = T'R_0 T$$

This is the desired matrix; performing two matrix multiplications gives:

$$R = \begin{bmatrix} \cos \varphi & \sin \varphi & 0 \\ -\sin \varphi & \cos \varphi & 0 \\ c_1 & c_2 & 1 \end{bmatrix}$$

where c_1 and c_2 are the following constants:

$$c_1 = x_0 - x_0 \cos \varphi + y_0 \sin \varphi$$
$$c_2 = y_0 - x_0 \sin \varphi - y_0 \cos \varphi$$

2.4 WINDOWS AND VIEWPORTS

In many situations we have to draw objects whose dimensions are given in units completely incompatible with our screen co-ordinate system. A building may be a hundred times larger than its image we want to produce. A molecule, on the other hand, is much smaller in reality than in a picture. Finally there are applications where the object to be drawn is not a concrete one but a graphical representation of relations between quantities, as, for example, in Fig. 2.6, where the profits of a certain company at the beginning of the twentieth century are shown.

Problem-oriented dimensions are expressed in so-called *world co-ordinates*. In Fig. 2.6 the numbers 1901, 1902, 1903, 1904 and 50 000, 100 000, 150 000, 200 000 and 250 000 are world co-ordinates. We now introduce the concept of a *window*; this is a rectangle surrounding the object (or a part of it) that we wish to draw, as shown in Fig. 2.6. The sides of a window are parallel to the x- and the y-axis. To avoid confusion in what follows, it is most important to note that a window is more closely related to the object than to the image to be produced. If, as usual, we introduce a horizontal x-axis and a vertical y-axis, the window in Fig. 2.6 is completely determined by:

$$x_{min} = 1898$$
$$x_{max} = 1908$$
$$y_{min} = -150\ 000$$
$$y_{max} = 325\ 000$$

We see that the dimensions and the position of the window are expressed in world

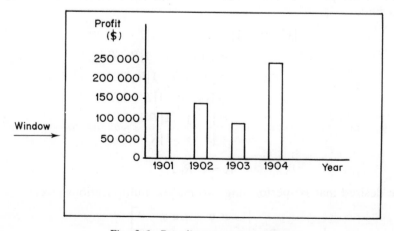

Fig. 2.6. Bar diagram in a window

co-ordinates. This may surprise the reader, since the window was introduced to specify what we wish to see in the picture and, at first sight, a number of inches seems more natural to achieve this than, for example, a fictitious profit of $-\$150\,000$, as given here for y_{min}. However, expressing windows in world co-ordinates is customary and very convenient in practice.

To produce the desired picture a rectangular region of the screen must be given as well. This region is called a *viewport*. It is specified in a way similar to that of a window, that is, by the minimum and maximum values of the X- and Y-co-ordinates, but now they are screen co-ordinates. We shall denote them by capital letters X and Y. A typical viewport specification is:

$$X_{min} = 1.5$$
$$X_{max} = 7.5$$
$$Y_{min} = 1.0$$
$$Y_{max} = 6.0$$

The window will now be mapped to the viewport. For example, a given world co-ordinate $x = 1898$ will be converted to the screen co-ordinate $X = 1.5$. First, the scale factors f_x and f_y are calculated:

$$f_x = \frac{X_{max} - X_{min}}{x_{max} - x_{min}}$$

$$f_y = \frac{Y_{max} - Y_{min}}{y_{max} - y_{min}}$$

In our example we find $f_x = 0.6$ and $f_y = 0.0000105$. Then the distance $X - X_{min}$ of an image point to the left viewport edge is found as f_x times the corresponding distance $x - x_{min}$ of the original point to the left window edge, and $Y - Y_{min}$ is found similarly, which leads to:

$$X = X_{min} + f_x \cdot (x - x_{min})$$
$$Y = Y_{min} + f_y \cdot (y - y_{min})$$

$$(2.12)$$

We conclude this section with three remarks.

(1) The window may or may not encompass the complete object. If it does not, the parts of the object which are outside the window must not be drawn but they are to be cut off. This activity is known as *clipping*; it will be dealt with in Section 2.5.

(2) In general the scale factors f_x and f_y are different. For a bar diagram this is just what we want, but it is not in cases where angles in the picture are to be the same as those in the object. We can then use the smaller of f_x and f_y for both scale factors. It is then recommended to replace Eq. (2.12) with formulae based on the centres of the window and the viewport. This will be shown in Section 2.6.

(3) The dimensions and the position of the window are not always known beforehand. In Section 2.6 they will be calculated instead of being specified by the user.

2.5 LINE CLIPPING

In this section we shall assume world co-ordinates and screen co-ordinates to be identical; in other words, the window and the viewport will coincide. The term 'window' in this section could therefore be replaced with 'viewport' everywhere. It is, however, customary to clip against a window rather than against a viewport, and we shall conform to this usage.

Figure 2.7 shows a rectangle ABCD which is a window. All line segments to be drawn must be inside the window; in other words, if a line segment is to be drawn, those parts that are outside the window must be clipped. We wish the clipping process to be done automatically. Commands to draw triangle PQR in Fig. 2.7 are to be interpreted as commands to draw the line segments P'P, PQ and QQ'. Rectangle ABCD is drawn beforehand, so the complete polygon PQQ'P' is drawn instead of triangle PQR.

Since only the three points P, Q and R are given, the co-ordinate pair $(x_{P'}, y_{P'})$ has to be derived from (x_P, y_P) and (x_R, y_R). In Fig. 2.7 we see that the slope of PR can be expressed in two ways, which gives the following equation:

$$\frac{y_{P'} - y_P}{x_{P'} - x_P} = \frac{y_R - y_P}{x_R - x_P}$$

We combine this with

$$y_{P'} = y_{max}$$

and find

$$x_{P'} = x_P + \frac{(x_R - x_P)(y_{max} - y_P)}{y_R - y_P}$$

We see that the co-ordinates of P' can easily be calculated if it is known that endpoint P is inside the window and endpoint $R(x_R, y_R)$ satisfies:

$$x_{min} < x_R < x_{max}$$
$$y_R > y_{max}$$

There are, however, many more cases to be considered. The logical decisions

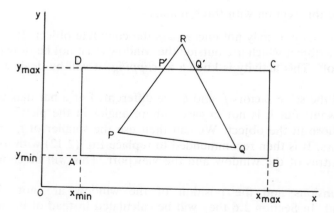

Fig. 2.7. Triangle to be clipped

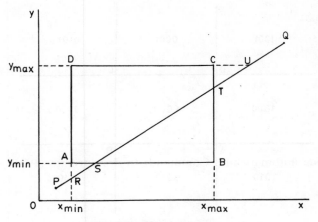

Fig. 2.8. Clipping in steps

needed to find this out make line clipping an interesting topic from an algorithmic point of view. In Fig. 2.8 it is clearly not sufficient to clip line segment PQ against line CD. Cohen and Sutherland developed an algorithm for line clipping, which is presented in Pascal by Newman and Sproull (1979). We shall express this algorithm in the C language.

With any point P(x, y) we associate a four-bit code

$$b_3 \ b_2 \ b_1 \ b_0$$

where b_i is either 0 or 1 ($i = 0, 1, 2, 3$). This code contains useful information about the position of P relative to window ABCD. In C the (truth) values of expressions as $x < x_{min}$ are 1 for *true* and 0 for *false*. Using this, we write

$$b3 = (x < xmin) \qquad /* \ P \ to \ the \ left \ of \ AD \quad */;$$
$$b2 = (x > xmax) \qquad /* \ P \ to \ the \ right \ of \ BC \ */;$$
$$b1 = (y < ymin) \qquad /* \ P \ below \ AB \qquad\qquad */;$$
$$b0 = (y > ymax) \qquad /* \ P \ above \ CD \qquad\qquad */;$$

Only nine out of the sixteen possible bit-configurations actually occur, and these are shown in Fig. 2.9.

In C such a code value is delivered by the following function:

```
int code(x, y) float x, y;
{return(x < xmin) ≪ 3 | (x > xmax) ≪ 2 | (y < ymin) ≪ 1 | (y > ymax);
}
```

To understand this, we must know that $b \ll n$ is what we obtain if the bitstring b is shifted n positions to the left. Besides ≪ for left shift there is a bit operator written as |, for *bitwise or*. This operator must not be confused with the logical *or*-operator written as ‖. A less efficient version of the above expression in the return statement would be:

$$(x < xmin)*8 + (x > xmax)*4 + (y < ymin)*2 + (y > ymax)$$

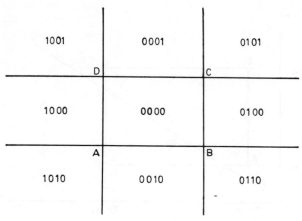

Fig. 2.9. Code values

The latter version is merely given to understand the former.

The above function *code* will be used in the function *clip*, whose task is to analyse a given line segment P_1P_2 and to draw that part of this line segment that is in window ABCD, if such a part exists. It works as follows.

As long as at least one of the codes for P_1 and P_2 contains a 1-bit, either P_1 or P_2 is moved from outside the window to one of its edges or to an extension of such an edge. In the latter case the point is still outside the window, so another move will be necessary. In Fig. 2.8, for example, a move from P to R has to be followed by one from R to S. Then at the other end of the line segment clipping may be necessary, as Fig. 2.8 shows. Thus clipping is a repetitive process; in each step the distance between P_1 and P_2 decreases. The process terminates as soon as both points are no longer outside the window. Line segment P_1P_2 thus obtained is then drawn. There is, however, another important case in which the loop is to terminate, namely if both P_1 and P_2 are outside the window and at the same side of the window. This case may not apply initially but may arise during the clipping process. If the endpoints of a line segment are outside a window, the line segments may or may not intersect the window, as Figs 2.8 and 2.10 show. In Fig. 2.10, initially P_1 and P_2 are not both below the window. After some steps in the clipping process Q and S are

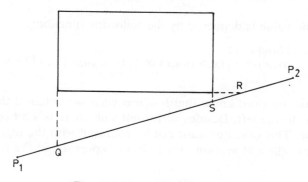

Fig. 2.10. Line outside window

the new positions of P_1 and P_2, respectively. Since both points are now below the window it can be decided that nothing has to be drawn at all. Such decisions are made on the basis of the value of $code(x1, y1)$ and $code(x2, y2)$. The points P_1 and P_2 are at the same side of the window if and only if their codes have a 1 in the same position. For the three points P_1, Q, S the third bit from the left $(b1)$ in their codes is 1, whereas this bit is 0 for point P_2. This is why P_2 has to be moved to S. Moving P_1 to Q is not necessary but this move is performed because it does no harm and keeps the algorithm simple.

Like the bitwise *or*-operator |, explained earlier, the C language offers the bitwise *and*-operator, written as &. Note that the logical versions of these operators are || and &&. Bit operators (such as & and |) give bitstrings as results; a logical operation gives a single 1 or 0, being the representation of *true* and *false,* respectively. Not only 1 but any value unequal to zero acts as *true* if it is used in a logical context. Therefore the loop construction

$$while \ (c1 \mid c2) \ . \ . \ .$$

will execute the actions indicated by . . . , as long as evaluation of $c1 \mid c2$ gives a bitstring containing a 1-bit, that is, as long as there is a 1-bit anywhere in $c1$ or $c2$. On the other hand, the statement

$$if \ (c1 \ \& \ c2) \ return;$$

causes a direct return from the function, if and only if the bitstring value of $c1 \ \& \ c2$ contains a 1-bit, that is, if and only if both $c1$ and $c2$ have a 1-bit in the same position. The complete function *clip* is shown at the bottom of the following program, which clips concentric pentagons.

```
/* CLIPDEMO:                                                       */
/* Demonstration of the Cohen & Sutherland line-clipping           */
/* algorithm                                                       */
#include <math.h>
float xmin=1.0, xmax=7.0, ymin=2.0, ymax=6.0;

main()
{ int i;
  float r, pi, alpha, phi0, phi, x0, y0, x1, y1, x2, y2;
  pi=4.0*atan(1.0); alpha=72.0*pi/180.0; phi0=0.0;
  x0=4.0; y0=4.0;
  initgr();
  /* The window is now drawn: */
  move(xmin, ymin); draw(xmax, ymin); draw(xmax, ymax);
  draw(xmin, ymax); draw(xmin, ymin);
  /* As far as permitted by the boundaries of the window, */
  /* 20 concentric regular pentagons are drawn:           */
  for (r=0.5; r<10.5; r+=0.5)
  { x2=x0+r*cos(phi0); y2=y0+r*sin(phi0);
    for (i=1; i<=5; i++)
    { phi=phi0+i*alpha;
      x1=x2; y1=y2;
      x2=x0+r*cos(phi); y2=y0+r*sin(phi);
      clip(x1, y1, x2, y2);
    }
  }
  endgr();
}
```

```
int code(x, y) float x, y;
{ return (x<xmin)<<3 : (x>xmax)<<2 : (y<ymin)<<1 : (y>ymax);
}

clip(x1, y1, x2, y2) float x1, y1, x2, y2;
{ int c1=code(x1, y1), c2=code(x2, y2); float dx, dy;
  while (c1:c2)
  { if (c1&c2) return;
    dx=x2-x1; dy=y2-y1;
    if (c1)
    { if (c1 & 8) { y1 += dy*(xmin-x1)/dx; x1=xmin; } else
      if (c1 & 4) { y1 += dy*(xmax-x1)/dx; x1=xmax; } else
      if (c1 & 2) { x1 += dx*(ymin-y1)/dy; y1=ymin; } else
      if (c1 & 1) { x1 += dx*(ymax-y1)/dy; y1=ymax; }
      c1=code(x1, y1);
    } else
    { if (c2 & 8) { y2 += dy*(xmin-x2)/dx; x2=xmin; } else
      if (c2 & 4) { y2 += dy*(xmax-x2)/dx; x2=xmax; } else
      if (c2 & 2) { x2 += dx*(ymin-y2)/dy; y2=ymin; } else
      if (c2 & 1) { x2 += dx*(ymax-y2)/dy; y2=ymax; }
      c2=code(x2, y2);
    }
  }
  move(x1, y1); draw(x2, y2);
}
```

Figure 2.11 shows the output of this program.

Fig. 2.11. Output of program CLIPDEMO

2.6 ADJUSTING SIZE AND POSITION AUTOMATICALLY

To have a picture drawn within the boundaries of a viewport we can first clip it against a given window, as in Section 2.5, and then map the window and its contents to the viewport, as in Section 2.4. For many applications this procedure is satisfactory. In this section our approach will differ from this in the following respects:

(1) The object will be completely drawn, so no clipping will take place.
(2) The window will be calculated rather than specified.
(3) In mapping from window to viewport the same scale factor will be applied to the horizontal and the vertical directions.

Point (1) requires that the object be finite. For most applications this will be no severe restriction but it will exclude landscapes. Point (2) can be realized by scanning the object data twice. During the first scan the window boundaries x_{min}, x_{max}, y_{min} and y_{max} are determined. The drawing will be produced during the second scan. We shall use a file on disk for this purpose to avoid trouble due to memory limitations. Point (3) implies that each triangle in the picture will be similar to its original triangle in the object, which means that the mapping leaves angles unaltered.

Suppose that we are given the triangle PQR of Fig. 2.12. The relevant world co-ordinates are:

$$x_P = 1.0 \qquad x_Q = 1.5 \qquad x_R = 1.2$$
$$y_P = 0.8 \qquad y_Q = 0.9 \qquad y_R = 1.1$$

This will lead to a calculated window with characteristics:

$$x_{min} = 1.0 \qquad x_{max} = 1.5$$
$$y_{min} = 0.8 \qquad y_{max} = 1.1$$

Notice that extreme object points are now on the window boundaries, which was not the case in Section 2.4. To have some blank space at the four sides of our screen or

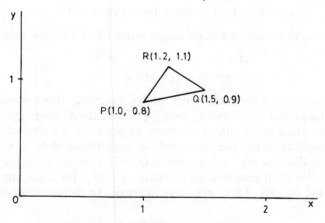

Fig. 2.12. An object to be adjusted

paper we shall have to specify a viewport that is somewhat smaller than it would otherwise have been. For example, we can set $X_{min} = 0.2$ instead of 0.0. Our viewport is completely determined if we choose, for example:

$$X_{min} = 0.2 \qquad X_{max} = 8.2$$
$$Y_{min} = 0.5 \qquad Y_{max} = 6.5$$

As in Section 2.4, we calculate:

$$f_x = \frac{X_{max} - X_{min}}{x_{max} - x_{min}} = \frac{8.2 - 0.2}{1.5 - 1.0} = 16$$

$$f_y = \frac{Y_{max} - Y_{min}}{y_{max} - y_{min}} = \frac{6.5 - 0.5}{1.1 - 0.8} = 20$$

The smaller of f_x and f_y will now be our scale factor f. Recall that distances will be multiplied by the scale factor, so part of the picture would certainly have been outside the viewport if we had chosen a scale factor greater than f_x or f_y. In our example we have:

$$f = f_x = 16$$

It will be clear that this common scale factor causes the mapped triangle to fit exactly in the viewport in the x-direction but not so for the y-direction, where blank space is to be added. We wish to distribute this blank space equally between the lower and the upper part of the viewport. This is accomplished by using the central value Y_C instead of the minimum value Y_{min}, as in Section 2.4, to calculate the constant c_2. The value of c_1 is determined similarly:

$$x_C = 0.5(x_{min} + x_{max}) = 0.5(1.0 + 1.5) = 1.25$$
$$y_C = 0.5(y_{min} + y_{max}) = 0.5(0.8 + 1.1) = 0.95$$

$$X_C = 0.5(X_{min} + X_{max}) = 0.5(0.2 + 8.2) = 4.2$$
$$Y_C = 0.5(Y_{min} + Y_{max}) = 0.5(0.5 + 6.5) = 3.5$$

$$c_1 = X_C - f \cdot x_C = 4.2 - 16 \times 1.25 = -15.8$$
$$c_2 = Y_C - f \cdot y_C = 3.5 - 16 \times 0.95 = -11.7$$

For any point (x, y) of the object its image point (X, Y) is now calculated as:

$$X = f \cdot x + c_1 = 16x - 15.8$$
$$Y = f \cdot y + c_2 = 16y - 11.7$$

We shall now develop a program which draws a picture whose window cannot be specified beforehand and a number of new aspects of the C language will appear in this example. We shall use random numbers to generate a curve of unpredictable shape and size and, as usual, the curve will be approximated by a great many line segments. Automatic scaling and positioning will relieve us from a practically impossible task. We shall generate co-ordinates x and y for each line segment and write them to a file on disk. More precisely, we write so-called *structures,* containing the triples

x   y   code

where (x, y) is the point a pen has to go to, and *code* is either 0 or 1, meaning 'pen up' or 'pen down', respectively. In other words,

$$x \ y \ 0 \quad \text{means} \quad move(X, Y)$$
$$x \ y \ 1 \quad \text{means} \quad draw(X, Y)$$

where X and Y are screen co-ordinates corresponding to the world co-ordinates x and y. In this example we shall use a special program which generates a curve and writes triples in the file *A.SCRATCH*. The execution of this program is to be followed by a run of the general plot program *GENPLOT*, which reads the triples twice; first, to determine the window characteristics *xmin, xmax, ymin, ymax* and second, to perform the actual move and draw operations, using screen co-ordinates X and Y, derived from the world co-ordinates x and y.

In the curve-generation program we start in the origin O and move one unit of distance at a time. There is always a current direction φ and a current turning angle α. Initially they are both set to zero. Before each step, α is increased by a randomly chosen angle between $-6°$ and $+6°$ (integer). The new turning angle α is then added to the current direction φ to find a new direction. We shall limit the curvature and reduce the chance of looping in circles. Therefore the above algorithm is modified in that we set α equal to zero as soon as its absolute value is greater than 15°. The following program generates the curve.

```
/* CURVGEN: Generation of a random curve */
#include <math.h>
main()
{ int i, N=500;
  float x=0.0, y=0.0, x0, y0, phi, direction();
  pfopen(); pmove(x, y);
  for (i=1; i<=N; i++)
  { x0=x; y0=y;
    phi=direction();
    x=x0+cos(phi); y=y0+sin(phi);
    pdraw(x, y);
  }
  pfclose();
}

float direction()
{ static int phi=0, alpha=0, first=1;
  /* Static variables are initialized in the first call only! */
  float pi=3.1415926; long int seed;
  if (first) { first=0; time(&seed); srand((int)seed); }
  alpha+=rand()%13-6;
  if (abs(alpha)>15) alpha=0;
  phi+=alpha;
  return ((float)phi*pi/180.0);
}

#include <stdio.h>
FILE *fp;
struct {float xx; float yy; int ii;} s;

pfopen() { fp=fopen("a.scratch", "w"); } /* system dependent */

pmove(x, y) float x, y;
```

```
{ s. xx=x; s. yy=y; s. ii=0; /* 0 = pen up */
  fwrite(&s, sizeof s, 1, fp);
}

pdraw(x, y) float x, y;
{ s. xx=x; s. yy=y; s. ii=1; /* 1 = pen down */
  fwrite(&s, sizeof s, 1, fp);
}

pfclose() { fclose(fp); }
```

The function *direction* shows a call of the random initialization function *srand*. Its argument *seed* supplies a start value for random number generation. The function *time* is used to obtain a value for *seed* depending on the actual clock time. In this way we generate different curves if the program is run more than once. The function *rand* gives a large non-negative integer. This is converted to one of the integers $0, 1, \ldots, 12$ by taking the remainder after dividing it by 13. Thus

$$0 \leqslant rand(\ )\%13 \qquad \leqslant 12$$
$$-6 \leqslant rand(\ )\%13 - 6 \leqslant 6$$

More new C aspects concern input and output (I/O). Most I/O functions require the line *#include* ⟨*stdio.h*⟩, which 'includes' a so-called header file for standard I/O. In C we distinguish formatted and unformatted I/O. The following functions are used very often:

scanf:	formatted input from the terminal,
printf:	formatted output to the terminal,
fscanf:	formatted input from a file,
fprintf:	formatted output to a file,
fread:	unformatted input (from a file),
fwrite:	unformatted output (to a file).

Formatted I/O deals with readable characters; there is a line structure in the same way as on a printed page. Unformatted data on a file has the same structure as it has in memory; for example, an integer is represented by a fixed number of bits. We have used unformatted I/O for reasons of efficiency. A file is 'opened' by a call of the function *fopen*. Its second argument is either the string *"r"* to initiate reading or the string *"w"* for writing. (For unformatted I/O, some compilers require other strings than *"r"* or *"w"*.) Variable *s* is the structure containing the three numbers *x, y* and *code* that are to be written. A 'pointer' &*s* to this variable is the first argument of *fwrite*. We can regard &*s* as a notation for the address of *s*. The second argument *sizeof s* is the size of one structure *s* and the third argument 1 is the number or structures to be written. The fourth argument *fp* is the file pointer, obtained by the call of *fopen*.

We now turn to the general program which reads triples, determines the window, performs the conversion from world co-ordinates to screen co-ordinates and finally draws the picture within a given viewport. The corners of the viewport are drawn too, along with a dot in the middle of the bottom boundary so that in abstract pictures we can distinguish between bottom and top. (If the dot and the corners are not desired they can easily be erased.)

Notice that in this program the file *A.SCRATCH* is opened twice. Closing and opening has the effect of rewinding a file:

```
/* GENPLOT: A general adjusting and plotting program.      */
/* The file A.SCRATCH contains input data.                 */
#include <stdio.h>

main()
{ float x, y, xmin, xmax, ymin, ymax, X, Y, Xmin, Xmax,
          Ymin, Ymax, fx, fy, f, xC, yC, XC, YC, c1, c2;
  FILE *fp;
  struct {float xx; float yy; int ii;} s;
  fp=fopen("a.scratch", "r"); /* system dependent */
  xmin=ymin=1e30; xmax=ymax=-xmin;
  while (fread(&s, sizeof s, 1, fp))
  { x=s.xx; y=s.yy;
    if (x<xmin) xmin=x;
    if (x>xmax) xmax=x;
    if (y<ymin) ymin=y;
    if (y>ymax) ymax=y;
  }
  fclose(fp);
  init_viewport(&Xmin, &Xmax, &Ymin, &Ymax);
  fx=(Xmax-Xmin)/(xmax-xmin); fy=(Ymax-Ymin)/(ymax-ymin);
  f=(fx<fy?fx:fy);
  xC=0.5*(xmin+xmax); yC=0.5*(ymin+ymax);
  XC=0.5*(Xmin+Xmax); YC=0.5*(Ymin+Ymax);
  c1=XC-f*xC; c2=YC-f*yC;
  fp=fopen("a.scratch", "r"); /* system dependent */
  while (fread(&s, sizeof s, 1, fp))
  { x=s.xx; y=s.yy;
    X=f*x+c1; Y=f*y+c2;
    if (s.ii) draw(X, Y); else move(X, Y);
  }
  fclose(fp); endgr();
}

init_viewport(pXmin, pXmax, pYmin, pYmax)
  float *pXmin, *pXmax, *pYmin, *pYmax;
{ float Xmin, Xmax, Ymin, Ymax, eps=0.2;
  printf("Give viewport boundaries Xmin, Xmax, Ymin, Ymax\n");
  scanf("%f %f %f %f", &Xmin, &Xmax, &Ymin, &Ymax);
  /* Show the four viewport corners:   */
  initgr();
  move(Xmin, Ymin+eps); draw(Xmin, Ymin); draw(Xmin+eps, Ymin);
  move(Xmax-eps, Ymin); draw(Xmax, Ymin); draw(Xmax, Ymin+eps);
  move(Xmax, Ymax-eps); draw(Xmax, Ymax); draw(Xmax-eps, Ymax);
  move(Xmin+eps, Ymax); draw(Xmin, Ymax); draw(Xmin, Ymax-eps);
  move((Xmin+Xmax)/2, Ymin); draw((Xmin+Xmax)/2, Ymin);
  /* Dot in the middle of bottom boundary for orientation */
  *pXmin=Xmin; *pXmax=Xmax; *pYmin=Ymin; *pYmax=Ymax;
}
```

The arguments of the function *init_viewport* are pointers. The notation *float *pXmin* expresses that *$*pXmin$* is of type *float*, so *pXmin* is of type *pointer to float*. The unary operators & and $*$ are each other's inverses, so $pXmin = \&Xmin$ and $Xmin = *pXmin$. The output of this program is shown in Fig. 2.13.

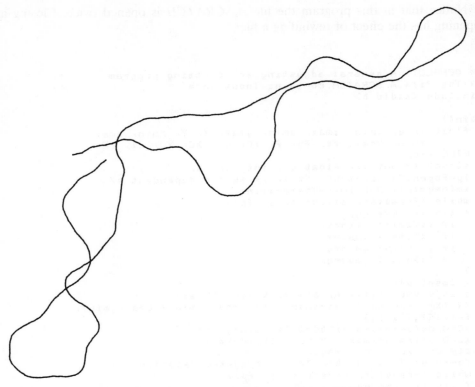

Fig. 2.13. Result of programs CURVGEN and GENPLOT

2.7 APPLICATIONS OF RECURSION

Many tasks can be formulated recursively. An example of such a task is:
With three given numbers x_C, y_C and r connect the points with co-ordinates

$$x_i = x_C + r \cos \varphi_i$$
$$y_i = y_C + r \sin \varphi_i$$
$$(i = 0, 1, 2, 3, 4, 5; \varphi_i = i \cdot 144°)$$

which will produce a star. Subsequently (and as part of the task!) perform a similar task five times, but now with the three given numbers:

$$x_{C'} = x_C + 2r \cos \varphi_j$$
$$y_{C'} = y_C + 2r \sin \varphi_j$$
$$r' = 0.5r$$
$$(j = 0, 1, 2, 3, 4; \varphi_j = 36° + j \cdot 72°)$$

The whole task is to be performed only if the given value r is at least 0.1.
For the initial or main task the three given numbers are $x_C = 0$, $y_C = 0$, $r = 1$. As

before, we shall use automatic size adjusting and positioning. Here is a program which performs the task described above:

```
/* STARS: Stars of various sizes */
#include <math.h>

main()
{ pfopen(); star(0.0, 0.0, 1.0); pfclose();
}

star(xC, yC, r) float xC, yC, r;
{ float phi, r_half, r_double,
        factor=0.0174533; /* factor = pi/180 */
  int i;
  if (r<0.1) return;
  pmove(xC+r, yC);
  for (i=1; i<=5; i++)
  { phi=i*144*factor;
    pdraw(xC+r*cos(phi), yC+r*sin(phi));
  }
  r_half=0.5*r; r_double=2*r;
  for (i=0; i<5; i++)
  { phi=(36+i*72)*factor;
    star(xC+r_double*cos(phi), yC+r_double*sin(phi), r_half);
  }
}


#include <stdio.h>
FILE *fp;
struct {float xx; float yy; int ii;} s;

pfopen() { fp=fopen("a.scratch", "w"); } /* system dependent */

pmove(x, y) float x, y;
{ s.xx=x; s.yy=y; s.ii=0; /* 0 = pen up */
  fwrite(&s, sizeof s, 1, fp);
}

pdraw(x, y) float x, y;
{ s.xx=x; s.yy=y; s.ii=1; /* 1 = pen down */
  fwrite(&s, sizeof s, 1, fp);
}

pfclose() { fclose(fp); }
```

This program, followed by the program *GENPLOT* of the previous section, will produce Fig. 2.14.

Our next example is known as Pythagoras's Tree. This tree is often shown as in Fig. 2.15. Each right-angled triangle in this tree has an angle of 45°. We shall again use random numbers in a rather general program: it can produce the tree of Fig. 2.15, but also less regular trees. The angles that are 45° in Fig. 2.15 will be randomly chosen between $(45 - delta)°$ and $(45 + delta)°$, where *delta* is given as input data, together with *n*, the recursion depth. The regular version of Fig. 2.15 was produced by choosing *delta* = 0 and *n* = 7. In the picture *n* is the number of triangles we encounter if we follow a path from the root to a leaf of the tree. The heart of the

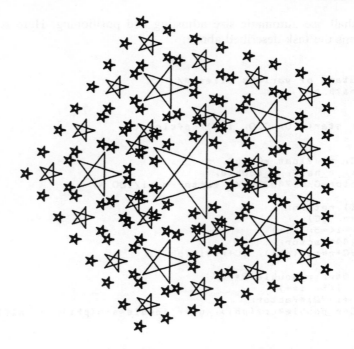

Fig. 2.14. Output of program STARS

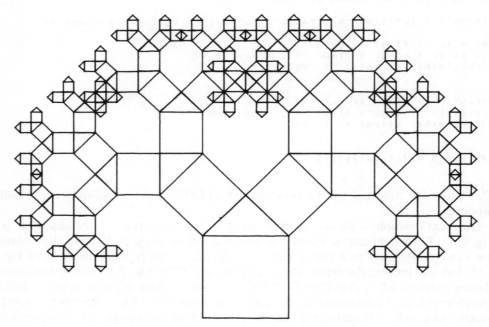

Fig. 2.15. Pythagoras's Tree, regular version

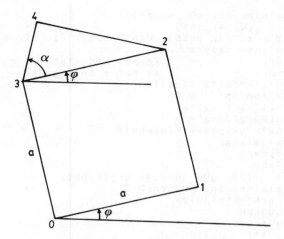

Fig. 2.16. Point numbering

program will be the recursive function *square_and_triangle,* with the recursion depth *n* as its first argument. If *n* is greater than zero, the task of *square_and_triangle* is, as its name indicates, to draw a square and a triangle on top of it, and subsequently invoke the same function twice with appropriate new arguments, the first of which is $n - 1$. The size and position of the square are fully determined by the four arguments x_0, y_0, *a* and *φ* (see Fig. 2.16). To draw the triangle we need the angle *α*. This angle, expressed in degrees, is equal to $45 + deviation$, where *deviation* is one of the integers $-delta, -delta + 1, \ldots, delta$, randomly chosen as in Section 2.6.

In Fig. 2.16 the relevant points are numbered 0, 1, 2, 3, 4. The co-ordinates x_0 and y_0 of point 0 are given. To find the co-ordinates of the other points we first consider the much simpler situation with $φ = 0$, that is, where side 0 1 of the square is horizontal. In this situation, the co-ordinates of the points are easily found. They are stored in the arrays *x* and *y*. Then we rotate everything about point 0 through the angle *φ* in the same way as in Section 2.3. The results of the rotation are stored in the arrays *xx* and *yy*:

```
/* PYTH_TREE: Variants of the tree of Pythagoras   */
#include <math.h>
#define pi 3.1415927
int delta;
long int seed;

main()
{ int n;
  pfopen(); time(&seed); srand((int)seed);
  printf("Give angle delta in degrees (0 < delta < 45)\n");
  scanf("%d", &delta);
  printf("Give recursion depth n\n"); scanf("%d", &n);
  square_and_triangle(n, 0.0, 0.0, 1.0, 0.0);
  pfclose();
}
```

```
square_and_triangle(n, x0, y0, a, phi)
   int n; float x0, y0, a, phi;
{ float x[5], y[5], xx[5], yy[5], cphi, sphi, c1, c2, b, c,
        alpha, calpha, salpha;
  int i, deviation;                 /* phi and alpha in radians */
  if (n==0) return;                 /* delta in degrees         */
  deviation=rand()%(2*delta+1)-delta;
  alpha=(45+deviation)*pi/180.0;
  x[0]=x[3]=x0; x[1]=x[2]=x0+a;
  y[0]=y[1]=y0; y[2]=y[3]=y0+a;
  calpha=cos(alpha); salpha=sin(alpha);
  c=a*calpha; b=a*salpha;
  x[4]=x[3]+c*calpha;
  y[4]=y[3]+c*salpha;
  /* Rotation about (x0, y0) through angle phi;  */
  /* this was explained in Section 2-3           */
  cphi=cos(phi); sphi=sin(phi);
  c1=x0-x0*cphi+y0*sphi;
  c2=y0-x0*sphi-y0*cphi;
  for (i=0; i<5; i++)
  { xx[i]=x[i]*cphi-y[i]*sphi+c1;
    yy[i]=x[i]*sphi+y[i]*cphi+c2;
  }
  pmove(xx[3], yy[3]);
  for (i=0; i<5; i++) pdraw(xx[i], yy[i]);
  pdraw(xx[2], yy[2]);
  square_and_triangle(n-1, xx[3], yy[3], c, phi+alpha);
  square_and_triangle(n-1, xx[4], yy[4], b, phi+alpha-0.5*pi);
}

#include <stdio.h>
FILE *fp;
struct {float xx; float yy; int ii;} s;

pfopen() { fp=fopen("a.scratch", "w"); } /* system dependent */

pmove(x, y) float x, y;
{ s.xx=x; s.yy=y; s.ii=0; /* 0 = pen up */
  fwrite(&s, sizeof s, 1, fp);
}

pdraw(x, y) float x, y;
{ s.xx=x; s.yy=y; s.ii=1; /* 1 = pen down */
  fwrite(&s, sizeof s, 1, fp);
}

pfclose() { fclose(fp); }
```

Again, the file *A.SCRATCH*, produced by this program, has to be processed by program *GENPLOT* of Section 2.5. The graphical output thus produced, with *delta* = 30 and *n* = 7, is shown in Fig. 2.17.

2.8   CURVE FITTING

In computer aided design (CAD) and computer aided manufacturing (CAM) it is often required to construct a smooth curve or a smooth surface through some given points. Here we shall deal with two dimensions only, so we shall restrict ourselves to

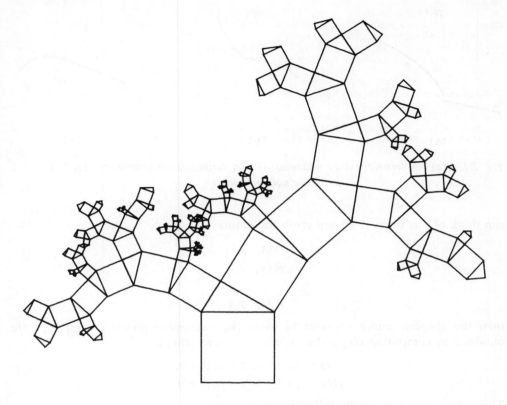

Fig. 2.17. Typical output of program PYTH_TREE

curves in the xy-plane. Curve fitting will be a sound base for surface fitting at a later stage.

Out of several methods available we choose the B-spline form. A sequence of points is given, and between two successive points of the sequence a cubic curve is constructed, based on the position of four points, namely the two just mentioned and their two neighbouring points. The B-spline form yields smoother curves than other methods, at the price that the curves will not exactly pass through the given points. The smoothness of a curve is mathematically expressed in terms of the continuity of its parametric representations $x(t)$ and $y(t)$ and their derivatives. B-spline curves have the property that even the second derivatives $x''(t)$ and $y''(t)$ are continuous in the points where two successive curve segments meet. In Fig. 2.18 we can see how curves appear if their zeroth, first or second derivatives are not continuous in some point. Although the curve in Fig. 2.18(c) is generally considered smooth it does not obey the strict rules imposed by the B-spline method.

After this informal discussion we wish to see this method in action. We shall use a parametric representation of curves. Any point of a curve segment between two successive given points P and Q will have co-ordinates $x(t)$ and $y(t)$, where t increases from 0 to 1 if the curve segment is followed from point P to point Q. We

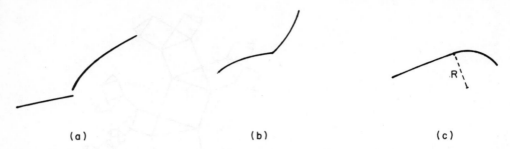

(a)   (b)   (c)

Fig. 2.18. (a) *0th derivative not continuous*; (b) *1st derivative not continuous*; (c) *2nd derivative not continuous*

can think of t as time. If we are given the points

$$P_0(x_0, y_0)$$
$$P_1(x_1, y_1)$$
$$\vdots$$
$$P_n(x_n, y_n)$$

then the B-spline curve segment between two successive points P_i and P_{i+1} are obtained by computing $x(t)$ and $y(t)$, where t grows from 0 to 1:

$$x(t) = \{(a_3t + a_2)t + a_1\}t + a_0$$
$$y(t) = \{(b_3t + b_2)t + b_1\}t + b_0$$

These equations contain the following coefficients:

$$\begin{aligned}
a_3 &= (-x_{i-1} + 3x_i - 3x_{i+1} + x_{i+2})/6 \\
a_2 &= (x_{i-1} - 2x_i + x_{i+1})/2 \\
a_1 &= (-x_{i-1} + x_{i+1})/2 \\
a_0 &= (x_{i-1} + 4x_i + x_{i+1})/6
\end{aligned} \tag{2.13}$$

and b_3, b_2, b_1, b_0 are derived from y_{i-1}, y_i, y_{i+1}, y_{i+2} in a similar manner. The formulae above are suited for efficient computation. The value of $x(t)$ is given according to Horner's rule rather than in the usual notation for a polynomial. The coefficients a_3, a_2, a_1, a_0 are computed only once for each of the curve segments, which is most important, since we wish to compute $x(t)$ and $y(t)$ a great many times on a single curve segment.

   To obtain some insight into the properties of the curve in the points where two segments meet we can investigate the function $x(t)$ and its first and second derivatives for the values $t = 0$ and $t = 1$ ($y(t)$ having similar properties):

$$x(0) = a_0 = (x_{i-1} + 4x_i + x_{i+1})/6$$
$$x(1) = a_3 + a_2 + a_1 + a_0$$

Using Eqs (2.13) and simplifying we have

$$x(1) = (x_i + 4x_{i+1} + x_{i+2})/6$$

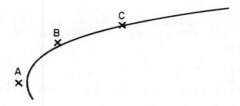

Fig. 2.19. Three successive points

We observe that $x(0)$ is not exactly equal to the x-co-ordinate x_i of P_i, but that it is also influenced by the points P_{i-1} and P_{i+1}. In Fig. 2.19 point B is the endpoint of segment AB but also the startpoint of BC. From the first point of view we have

$$A = P_i, \qquad B = P_{i+1}, \qquad C = P_{i+2}$$
$$x_B^* = x(1) = (x_A + 4x_B + x_C)/6$$

where x_B^* denotes the computed x-value at B. Viewed from segment BC, however, we have

$$A = P_{i+1}, \qquad B = P_i, \qquad C = P_{i+1}$$
$$x_B^* = x(0) = (x_A + 4x_B + x_C)/6$$

We have found that both ways of calculating x give the same answer, which means that $x(t)$ is continuous in B.

Differentiating $x(t)$ twice, we find $x'(t)$ and $x''(t)$. We can then substitute $t = 0$ and $t = 1$ in these functions as we did in $x(t)$. It is then seen that they too are continuous in point B. Since $y(t)$ and its first and second derivatives are continuous as well, it will now be clear that B-spline curves are very smooth.

For any curve segment between P_i and P_{i+1} we also use the points P_{i-1} and P_{i+2}. This implies that the first curve segment will be between P_1 and P_2, and the final one between P_{n-2} and P_{n-1}. Thus the start and the end points of the entire curve will be near P_1 and P_{n-1} and not near P_0 and P_n. The following program reads the numbers

$$n$$

x_0	y_0
x_1	y_1
$\vdots$	$\vdots$
x_n	y_n

from the file *CURV.DAT*. In the output each of the $n + 1$ points are plotted in the form of a cross. Then the B-spline curve is drawn:

```
/* CURVFIT: Curve fitting using B splines */
#include <stdio.h>
#define MAX 100
#define N 30
```

```
main()
{ float x[MAX], y[MAX], eps=0.04, X, Y, t, xA, xB, xC, xD,
         yA, yB, yC, yD, a0, a1, a2, a3, b0, b1, b2, b3;
  int n, i, j, first;
  FILE *fp;
  fp=fopen("curv.dat", "r");
  fscanf(fp, "%d", &n);
  for (i=0; i<=n; i++) fscanf(fp, "%f %f", x+i, y+i);
  initgr();
  /* Mark the given points:  */
  for (i=0; i<=n; i++)
  { X=x[i]; Y=y[i];
    move(X-eps, Y-eps); draw(X+eps, Y+eps);
    move(X+eps, Y-eps); draw(X-eps, Y+eps);
  }
  first=1;
  for (i=1; i<n-1; i++)
  { xA=x[i-1]; xB=x[i]; xC=x[i+1]; xD=x[i+2];
    yA=y[i-1]; yB=y[i]; yC=y[i+1]; yD=y[i+2];
    a3=(-xA+3*(xB-xC)+xD)/6.0; b3=(-yA+3*(yB-yC)+yD)/6.0;
    a2=(xA-2*xB+xC)/2.0;       b2=(yA-2*yB+yC)/2.0;
    a1=(xC-xA)/2.0;            b1=(yC-yA)/2.0;
    a0=(xA+4*xB+xC)/6.0;       b0=(yA+4*yB+yC)/6.0;
    for (j=0; j<=N; j++)
    { t=(float)j/(float)N;
      X=((a3*t+a2)*t+a1)*t+a0;
      Y=((b3*t+b2)*t+b1)*t+b0;
      if (first) { first=0; move(X, Y);} else draw(X, Y);
    }
  }
  endgr(); fclose(fp);
}
```

The following data

20	
.75	1.4
.5	1
.75	.6
1.5	.4
2.25	.7
2.5	.9
3	.85
5	.75
6.25	.8
6.5	.85
6.5	1
6.5	1.15
6.25	1.2
5	1.25
3	1.15
2.5	1.1
2.25	1.3
1.5	1.6
.75	1.4
.5	1
.75	.6

in file *CURV.DAT* will produce the output of Fig. 2.20.

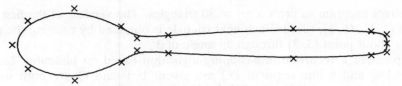

Fig. 2.20. Output of program CURVFIT

EXERCISES

2.1 Write a program to draw a set of N ellipses whose parametric equations are:

$$x = x_0 + (iR/N) \cos \varphi$$
$$y = y_0 + ((N - i)R/N) \sin \varphi$$

Choose fixed values x_0, y_0, R, N; for example, $x_0 = 4$, $y_0 = 3.5$, $R = 3$, $N = 40$. Let i range from 1 to $N - 1$. For each $i$value, let φ successively have the values $0°, 6°, 12°, \ldots, 360°$.

Fig. 2.21. Tree

2.2   Write a program to draw a set of 30 triangles. The vertices of the first triangle
      are $(1, 1)$, $(6, 1)$, $(3, 5)$. Each next triangle is obtained by rotating the previous
      one about point $(3, 3)$ through an angle of $3°$.

2.3   Implement a recursive line-clipping algorithm based on bisection. Suppose a
      window and a line segment PQ are given. If P and Q are both inside the
      window, PQ can be drawn. This is also the case if one of these points is inside
      the window and the other is on a window edge. There are also some cases
      where we can easily decide that nothing is to be drawn. Invent these yourself.
      In all other cases, find point M in the middle of PQ and apply the same
      procedure recursively to PM and MQ. Choose a tolerance with respect to the
      window edges, and investigate the influence of this tolerance on the number of
      bisections.

2.4   Develop and implement an algorithm for clipping a line against a window
      which is a triangle.

2.5   Modify program *STARS* in Section 2.7 such that stars will not overlap.

2.6   Use random numbers to generate a sequence of, say, 30 points, and apply
      curve fitting to draw a curve (approximately) through these points.

2.7   Write a program which produces a more realistic tree than Fig. 2.17. An
      example is given in Fig. 2.21.

CHAPTER 3

Geometric tools for three-dimensional algorithms

3.1 VECTORS

A certain amount of mathematical knowledge is essential to understand and write programs for three-dimensional graphics. This book is not intended to be a textbook on mathematics, and the reader is assumed to be already familiar with the mathematical topics of this chapter, especially with vectors and determinants.

A *vector* is a directed line segment, characterized by its length and its direction only. Figure 3.1 shows two representations of the same vector $\mathbf{a} = \mathbf{PQ} = \mathbf{b} = \mathbf{RS}$. Thus a vector is not altered by a translation. In Fig. 3.2 the initial point of $\mathbf{b}$ is the terminal point of $\mathbf{a}$. Then the sum of $\mathbf{a}$ and $\mathbf{b}$ is defined as the vector $\mathbf{c}$ drawn from the initial point of $\mathbf{a}$ to the terminal point of $\mathbf{b}$, and we write

$$\mathbf{c} = \mathbf{a} + \mathbf{b}$$

The length of a vector $\mathbf{a}$, denoted by $|\mathbf{a}|$, is the distance between its initial and its terminal points. A vector with length zero is the zero vector, written $\mathbf{0}$. The notation $-\mathbf{a}$ is used for the vector that has length $|\mathbf{a}|$ and whose direction is opposite to $\mathbf{a}$. For any vector $\mathbf{a}$ and real number c, the vector $c\mathbf{a}$ has length $|c|\,|\mathbf{a}|$. If $\mathbf{a} = \mathbf{0}$ or $c = 0$, then $c\mathbf{a} = \mathbf{0}$, otherwise $c\mathbf{a}$ has the direction of $\mathbf{a}$ if $c > 0$ and the opposite direction if $c < 0$. For any vectors $\mathbf{u}$, $\mathbf{v}$, $\mathbf{w}$ and real numbers c, k we have:

$$\mathbf{u} + \mathbf{v} = \mathbf{v} + \mathbf{u}$$
$$(\mathbf{u} + \mathbf{v}) + \mathbf{w} = \mathbf{u} + (\mathbf{v} + \mathbf{w})$$
$$\mathbf{u} + \mathbf{0} = \mathbf{u}$$
$$\mathbf{u} + (-\mathbf{u}) = \mathbf{0}$$
$$c(\mathbf{u} + \mathbf{v}) = c\mathbf{u} + c\mathbf{v}$$
$$(c + k)\mathbf{u} = c\mathbf{u} + k\mathbf{u}$$
$$c(k\mathbf{u}) = (ck)\mathbf{u}$$
$$1\mathbf{u} = \mathbf{u}$$
$$0\mathbf{u} = \mathbf{0}$$

Figure 3.3 shows three unit vectors $\mathbf{i}$, $\mathbf{j}$, $\mathbf{k}$. They are mutually perpendicular and have length 1. Their directions are the positive directions of the co-ordinate axes. We say that $\mathbf{i}$, $\mathbf{j}$, $\mathbf{k}$ form a triple of orthogonal unit vectors. The co-ordinate system is right-handed, which means that if a rotation of $\mathbf{i}$ into the direction of $\mathbf{j}$ through $90°$ corresponds to turning a right-handed screw, then $\mathbf{k}$ has the direction in which the screw advances.

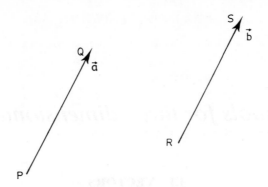

Fig. 3.1. Equal vectors

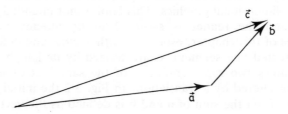

Fig. 3.2. Vector addition

We often choose the origin O of the co-ordinate system as the initial point of all vectors. Any vector **v** can be written as a linear combination of the unit vectors **i**, **j**, **k**:

$$\mathbf{v} = x\mathbf{i} + y\mathbf{j} + z\mathbf{k}$$

The real numbers x, y, z are the co-ordinates of the terminal point P of vector **v** = **OP**. We also write this vector **v** as either a row or a column:

$$\mathbf{v} = \begin{bmatrix} x & y & z \end{bmatrix} \quad \text{or} \quad \mathbf{v} = \begin{bmatrix} x \\ y \\ z \end{bmatrix}$$

The numbers x, y, z are sometimes called the elements of vector **v**.

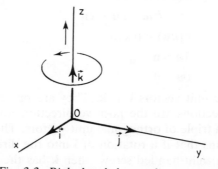

Fig. 3.3. Right-handed co-ordinate system

3.2 INNER PRODUCT

The *inner product, dot product* or *scalar product* of two vectors **a** and **b** is written **a** · **b** and is defined as

$$\mathbf{a} \cdot \mathbf{b} = |\mathbf{a}|\,|\mathbf{b}|\cos\gamma \quad \text{if} \quad \mathbf{a} \neq \mathbf{0} \quad \text{and} \quad \mathbf{b} \neq \mathbf{0}$$
$$\mathbf{a} \cdot \mathbf{b} = 0 \qquad\qquad \text{if} \quad \mathbf{a} = \mathbf{0} \quad \text{or} \quad \mathbf{b} = \mathbf{0} \tag{3.1}$$

where γ is the angle between **a** and **b**.

Applying this to the unit vectors **i**, **j**, **k** we find

$$\mathbf{i} \cdot \mathbf{i} = \mathbf{j} \cdot \mathbf{j} = \mathbf{k} \cdot \mathbf{k} = 1$$
$$\mathbf{i} \cdot \mathbf{j} = \mathbf{j} \cdot \mathbf{i} = \mathbf{j} \cdot \mathbf{k} = \mathbf{k} \cdot \mathbf{j} = \mathbf{k} \cdot \mathbf{i} = \mathbf{i} \cdot \mathbf{k} = 0 \tag{3.2}$$

Setting $\mathbf{b} = \mathbf{a}$ in Eqs (3.1) we have $\mathbf{a} \cdot \mathbf{a} = |\mathbf{a}|^2$, so

$$|\mathbf{a}| = \sqrt{|\mathbf{a} \cdot \mathbf{a}|}$$

Important properties of inner products are

$$c(k\mathbf{u} \cdot \mathbf{v}) = ck(\mathbf{u} \cdot \mathbf{v})$$
$$(c\mathbf{u} + k\mathbf{v}) \cdot \mathbf{w} = c\mathbf{u} \cdot \mathbf{w} + k\mathbf{v} \cdot \mathbf{w}$$
$$\mathbf{u} \cdot \mathbf{v} = \mathbf{v} \cdot \mathbf{u}$$
$$\mathbf{u} \cdot \mathbf{u} = 0 \quad \text{only if} \quad \mathbf{u} = \mathbf{0}$$

The inner product of two vectors $\mathbf{u} = [u_1\ u_2\ u_3]$ and $\mathbf{v} = [v_1\ v_2\ v_3]$ can be computed as

$$\mathbf{u} \cdot \mathbf{v} = u_1 v_1 + u_2 v_2 + u_3 v_3$$

This is proved by writing the right-hand side of

$$\mathbf{u} \cdot \mathbf{v} = (u_1\mathbf{i} + u_2\mathbf{j} + u_3\mathbf{k}) \cdot (v_1\mathbf{i} + v_2\mathbf{j} + v_3\mathbf{k})$$

as the sum of nine inner products and then applying Eqs (3.2).

3.3 DETERMINANTS

Before proceeding with vector products we shall pay some attention to determinants.

To solve the following system of two linear equations

$$\begin{cases} a_1 x + b_1 y = c_1 \\ a_2 x + b_2 y = c_2 \end{cases} \tag{3.3}$$

we multiply the first equation by b_2, the second by $-b_1$ and add, finding

$$(a_1 b_2 - a_2 b_1)x = b_2 c_1 - b_1 c_2$$

Then we multiply the first equation by $-a_2$, the second by a_1 and add again, finding

$$(a_1 b_2 - a_2 b_1)y = a_1 c_2 - a_2 c_1$$

If $a_1 b_2 - a_2 b_1$ is not zero, we can divide and find

$$x = \frac{b_2 c_1 - b_1 c_2}{a_1 b_2 - a_2 b_1}, \qquad y = \frac{a_1 c_2 - a_2 c_1}{a_1 b_2 - a_2 b_1} \tag{3.4}$$

The expression in the denominators is written in the form

$$\begin{vmatrix} a_1 & b_1 \\ a_2 & b_2 \end{vmatrix}$$

and then called a *determinant* of second order. Thus

$$\begin{vmatrix} a_1 & b_1 \\ a_2 & b_2 \end{vmatrix} = a_1 b_2 - a_2 b_1$$

With determinants the solution of Eqs (3.3) can be written

$$x = \frac{D_1}{D}, \qquad y = \frac{D_2}{D}, \quad (D \neq 0)$$

where

$$D = \begin{vmatrix} a_1 & b_1 \\ a_2 & b_2 \end{vmatrix} \qquad D_1 = \begin{vmatrix} c_1 & b_1 \\ c_2 & b_2 \end{vmatrix} \qquad D_2 = \begin{vmatrix} a_1 & c_1 \\ a_2 & c_2 \end{vmatrix}$$

Notice that D_i is obtained by replacing the ith column of D with the right-hand side of Eqs (3.3) ($i = 1$ or 2). This method of solving a system of linear equations is called Cramer's rule. It is not restricted to systems of two equations (although it would be very expensive in terms of computer time to apply the method to large systems). We define determinants of third order by the equation

$$D = \begin{vmatrix} a_1 & b_1 & c_1 \\ a_2 & b_2 & c_2 \\ a_3 & b_3 & c_3 \end{vmatrix} = a_1 \begin{vmatrix} b_2 & c_2 \\ b_3 & c_3 \end{vmatrix} - a_2 \begin{vmatrix} b_1 & c_1 \\ b_3 & c_3 \end{vmatrix} + a_3 \begin{vmatrix} b_1 & c_1 \\ b_2 & c_2 \end{vmatrix}$$

and determinants of fourth order by

$$D = \begin{vmatrix} a_1 & b_1 & c_1 & d_1 \\ a_2 & b_2 & c_2 & d_2 \\ a_3 & b_3 & c_3 & d_3 \\ a_4 & b_4 & c_4 & d_4 \end{vmatrix}$$

$$= a_1 \begin{vmatrix} b_2 & c_2 & d_2 \\ b_3 & c_3 & d_3 \\ b_4 & c_4 & d_4 \end{vmatrix} - a_2 \begin{vmatrix} b_1 & c_1 & d_1 \\ b_3 & c_3 & d_3 \\ b_4 & c_4 & d_4 \end{vmatrix} + a_3 \begin{vmatrix} b_1 & c_1 & d_1 \\ b_2 & c_2 & d_2 \\ b_4 & c_4 & d_4 \end{vmatrix} - a_4 \begin{vmatrix} b_1 & c_1 & d_1 \\ b_2 & c_2 & d_2 \\ b_3 & c_3 & d_3 \end{vmatrix}$$

and so on.

Determinants have many interesting properties, some of which are listed below.

(1) The value of a determinant is not altered if its rows are written as columns in the same order. For example:

$$\begin{vmatrix} a_1 & b_1 \\ a_2 & b_2 \end{vmatrix} = \begin{vmatrix} a_1 & a_2 \\ b_1 & b_2 \end{vmatrix}$$

(2) If any two rows (or two columns) are interchanged, the value of the

determinant is multiplied by -1. For example:

$$\begin{vmatrix} a_1 & b_1 & c_1 \\ a_2 & b_2 & c_2 \\ a_3 & b_3 & c_3 \end{vmatrix} = - \begin{vmatrix} a_1 & b_1 & c_1 \\ a_3 & b_3 & c_3 \\ a_2 & b_2 & c_2 \end{vmatrix}$$

(3) If any row (or column) is multiplied by a factor, the value of the determinant is multiplied by this factor. For example:

$$\begin{vmatrix} ca_1 & cb_1 \\ a_2 & b_2 \end{vmatrix} = c \begin{vmatrix} a_1 & b_1 \\ a_2 & b_2 \end{vmatrix}$$

(4) If a row (or a column) is altered by adding any constant multiple of any other row (or column) to it, the value of the determinant remains unaltered. For example:

$$\begin{vmatrix} a_1 & b_1 & c_1 \\ a_2 & b_2 & c_2 \\ a_3 + ka_1 & b_3 + kb_1 & c_3 + kc_1 \end{vmatrix} = \begin{vmatrix} a_1 & b_1 & c_1 \\ a_2 & b_2 & c_2 \\ a_3 & b_3 & c_3 \end{vmatrix}$$

(5) If a row (or column) is a linear combination of some other rows (or columns), the value of the determinant is zero. For example:

$$\begin{vmatrix} a_1 & b_1 & c_1 \\ a_2 & b_2 & c_2 \\ 3a_1 - 2a_2 & 3b_1 - 2b_2 & 3c_1 - 2c_2 \end{vmatrix} = 0$$

There are many useful applications of determinants. Determinant equations expressing geometrical properties are elegant and easy to remember. For example, the equation of the line in R_2 through the two points $P_1(x_1, y_1)$, $P_2(x_2, y_2)$ can be written

$$\begin{vmatrix} x & y & 1 \\ x_1 & y_1 & 1 \\ x_2 & y_2 & 1 \end{vmatrix} = 0 \tag{3.5}$$

This can be understood by observing first, that Eq. (3.5) is a special notation for a linear equation in x and y, and consequently represents a straight line in R_2, and second, that the co-ordinates of both P_1 and P_2 satisfy this equation, for if we write them in the first row we have two identical rows. Similarly, the plane in R_3 through the three points $P_1(x_1, y_1, z_1)$, $P_2(x_2, y_2, z_2)$, $P_3(x_3, y_3, z_3)$ has the equation

$$\begin{vmatrix} x & y & z & 1 \\ x_1 & y_1 & z_1 & 1 \\ x_2 & y_2 & z_2 & 1 \\ x_3 & y_3 & z_3 & 1 \end{vmatrix} = 0$$

3.4   VECTOR PRODUCT

The *vector product* or *cross-product* of two vectors **a** and **b** is written

$$\mathbf{a} \times \mathbf{b}$$

and is a vector **v** with the following properties. If $\mathbf{a} = c\mathbf{b}$ for some scalar c, then $\mathbf{v} = \mathbf{0}$. Otherwise the length of **v** is

$$|\mathbf{v}| = |\mathbf{a}|\,|\mathbf{b}|\,sin\,\gamma$$

where γ is the angle between **a** and **b**, and the direction of **v** is perpendicular to both **a** and **b** and is such that **a**, **b**, **v**, in that order, form a right-handed triple. The latter means that if **a** is rotated through an angle $\gamma < 180°$ into the direction of **b**, **v** has the direction of the advancement of a right-handed screw if turned in the same way. The following properties of vector products follow from this definition:

$$(k\mathbf{a}) \times \mathbf{b} \quad = k(\mathbf{a} \times \mathbf{b}) \text{ for any real number } k$$

$$\mathbf{a} \times (\mathbf{b} + \mathbf{c}) = \mathbf{a} \times \mathbf{b} + \mathbf{a} \times \mathbf{c}$$

$$\mathbf{a} \times \mathbf{b} \quad\quad = -\mathbf{b} \times \mathbf{a}$$

In general, $\mathbf{a} \times (\mathbf{b} \times \mathbf{c}) \neq (\mathbf{a} \times \mathbf{b}) \times \mathbf{c}$.

Using a right-handed orthogonal co-ordinate system as in Section 3.1, with unit vectors **i**, **j**, **k**, we have

$$\mathbf{i} \times \mathbf{i} = \mathbf{j} \times \mathbf{j} = \mathbf{k} \times \mathbf{k} = 0$$

$$\mathbf{i} \times \mathbf{j} = \mathbf{k}, \quad\quad \mathbf{j} \times \mathbf{k} = \mathbf{i}, \quad\quad \mathbf{k} \times \mathbf{i} = \mathbf{j}$$

$$\mathbf{j} \times \mathbf{i} = -\mathbf{k}, \quad\quad \mathbf{k} \times \mathbf{j} = -\mathbf{i}, \quad\quad \mathbf{i} \times \mathbf{k} = -\mathbf{j}$$

Using these vector products in the expansion of

$$\mathbf{a} \times \mathbf{b} = (a_1\mathbf{i} + a_2\mathbf{j} + a_3\mathbf{k}) \times (b_1\mathbf{i} + b_2\mathbf{j} + b_3\mathbf{k})$$

we obtain

$$\mathbf{a} \times \mathbf{b} = (a_2b_3 - a_3b_2)\mathbf{i} + (a_3b_1 - a_1b_3)\mathbf{j} + (a_1b_2 - a_2b_1)\mathbf{k}$$

which can be written

$$\mathbf{a} \times \mathbf{b} = \begin{vmatrix} a_2 & a_3 \\ b_2 & b_3 \end{vmatrix} \mathbf{i} + \begin{vmatrix} a_3 & a_1 \\ b_3 & b_1 \end{vmatrix} \mathbf{j} + \begin{vmatrix} a_1 & a_2 \\ b_1 & b_2 \end{vmatrix} \mathbf{k}$$

We rewrite this in a form that is very easy to remember:

$$\mathbf{a} \times \mathbf{b} = \begin{vmatrix} \mathbf{i} & \mathbf{j} & \mathbf{k} \\ a_1 & a_2 & a_3 \\ b_1 & b_2 & b_3 \end{vmatrix}$$

This is a mnemonic aid rather than a true determinant, since the element of the first row are vectors instead of numbers. If **a** and **b** are adjacent sides of a parallelogram, as in Fig. 3.4, the area of this parallelogram is the length of vector $\mathbf{a} \times \mathbf{b}$. This follows from $|\mathbf{a} \times \mathbf{b}| = |\mathbf{a}|\,|\mathbf{b}|\,sin\,\gamma$.

In Fig. 3.5 the vectors **a** and **b** lie in the plane through the x- and y-axes. We

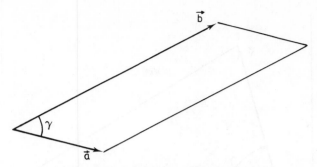

Fig. 3.4. *Parallelogram with area* $|\mathbf{a} \times \mathbf{b}|$

imagine a z-axis whose positive direction is out of paper towards the reader, so the co-ordinate system is right-handed. Then in three dimensions we have

$$\mathbf{a} = [a_1 \quad a_2 \quad 0], \qquad \mathbf{b} = [b_1 \quad b_2 \quad 0]$$

$$\mathbf{a} \times \mathbf{b} = \begin{vmatrix} \mathbf{i} & \mathbf{j} & \mathbf{k} \\ a_1 & a_2 & 0 \\ b_1 & b_2 & 0 \end{vmatrix} = \begin{vmatrix} a_1 & a_2 \\ b_1 & b_2 \end{vmatrix} \mathbf{k}$$

Thus the product vector $\mathbf{a} \times \mathbf{b}$ has the same direction as $\mathbf{k}$ if and only if the determinant

$$D = \begin{vmatrix} a_1 & a_2 \\ b_1 & b_2 \end{vmatrix}$$

is positive. This implies that the rotation of $\mathbf{a}$ into $\mathbf{b}$ through an angle less than 180° is counter-clockwise if and only if $D > 0$. We shall use this principle to determine whether the vertices A, B, C of a triangle, in that order, are traversed counter-clockwise.

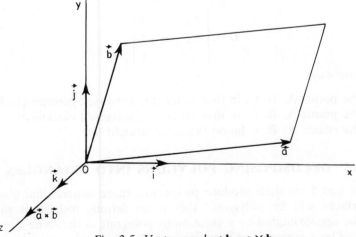

Fig. 3.5. *Vector product* $\mathbf{k} = \mathbf{a} \times \mathbf{b}$

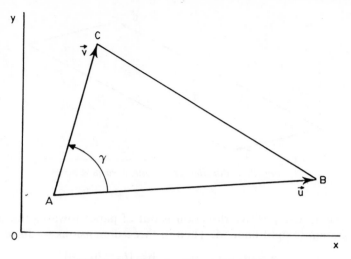

Fig. 3.6. A, B, C counter-clockwise

In Fig. 3.6 we have

$$\mathbf{u} = [u_1 \quad u_2] = \mathbf{AB}, \qquad \mathbf{v} = [v_1 \quad v_2] = \mathbf{AC}$$

$$D = \begin{vmatrix} x_A & y_A & 1 \\ x_B & y_B & 1 \\ x_C & y_C & 1 \end{vmatrix} = \begin{vmatrix} x_A & y_A & 1 \\ x_B - x_A & y_B - y_A & 0 \\ x_C - x_A & y_C - y_A & 0 \end{vmatrix}$$

$$= \begin{vmatrix} x_B - x_A & y_B - y_A \\ x_C - x_A & y_C - y_A \end{vmatrix} = \begin{vmatrix} u_1 & u_2 \\ v_1 & v_2 \end{vmatrix}$$

The vertices A, B, C, in that order, are traversed counter-clockwise if and only if $\mathbf{u}$ is rotated into the direction of $\mathbf{v}$ through an angle $\gamma < 180°$ counter-clockwise. This means that we can derive the rotation sense of A, B, C from the determinant

$$D = \begin{vmatrix} x_A & y_A & 1 \\ x_B & y_B & 1 \\ x_C & y_C & 1 \end{vmatrix}$$

in the following way:

If $D > 0$, the points A, B, C, in that order, are traversed counter-clockwise.
If $D < 0$, the points A, B, C, in that order, are traversed clockwise.
If $D = 0$, the points A, B, C lie on the same straight line.

3.5   DECOMPOSING POLYGONS INTO TRIANGLES

In Chapters 4 and 5 we shall produce pictures of three-dimensional objects whose boundary surfaces will be polygons. This is no serious restriction since curved surfaces can be approximated by a great many polygons in the same way as a curve is approximated by a sequence of line segments. Dealing with arbitrary polygons can

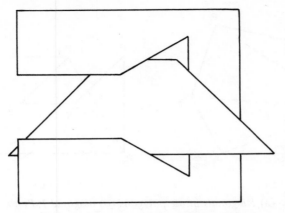

Fig. 3.7. Two polygons partly hiding each other

lead to quite complex situations, especially if visible and hidden line segments are distinguished. Figure 3.7 shows an example of such a situation.

If all interior angles of a polygon are less than 180° the polygon is called *convex*. In Fig. 3.8(b) the interior angle at vertex P is greater than 180°. We shall call such a vertex non-convex. All other vertices in Figs 3.8(a) and 3.8(b) are convex. If a polygon has at least one non-convex vertex, the polygon itself is said to be non-convex.

If A and B are two points on a convex polygon the entire line segment AB belongs to the polygon. For a non-convex polygon this may not be the case. Non-convexity of polygons is a source of complexity and so is their variable number of vertices. For these reasons we pay special attention to triangles. These obviously have a fixed number of vertices and they are always convex. They are also interesting in connection with arbitrary polygons because any polygon can be divided into a finite number of triangles. This will be the subject of this section.

Division of a convex polygon into triangles is extremely simple, as Fig. 3.9(a) shows. If the vertices are successively numbered $P_0, P_1, \ldots, P_{n-1}$, then drawing the diagonals $P_0P_2, P_0P_3, \ldots, P_0P_{n-2}$ is all that is needed. In a non-convex polygon such as in Fig. 3.9(b), however, this simple method will not work, since some of the diagonals $P_0P_2, P_0P_3, \ldots, P_0P_{n-2}$ may not completely lie inside the polygon. We shall now develop a program which reads the co-ordinates of a polygon's vertices

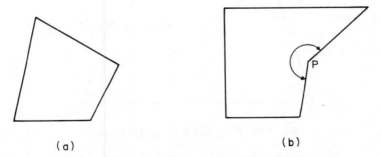

(a)   (b)

Fig. 3.8. (a) *Convex polygon*; (b) *non-convex polygon*

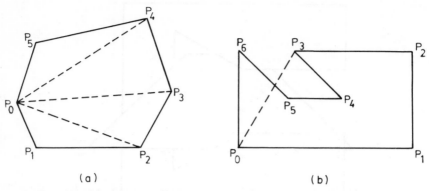

(a)   (b)

Fig. 3.9. (a) *Diagonals inside polygon*; (b) *diagonal P_0P_3 not usable*

and perform a division into triangles.[1] We shall require the vertices to be specified in a counter-clockwise order. For example, in Fig. 3.9(b) the sequence $P_4P_5P_6P_0P_1P_2P_3$ will do, but the sequence $P_6P_5P_4P_3P_2P_1P_0$ will not. For a polygon with n vertices the number n is given first, followed by the n co-ordinate pairs of successive vertices in counter-clockwise order. The output will be a drawing of the polygon in which diagonals are drawn, completely dividing the polygon into triangles. Before drawing the diagonal we have to ensure that the entire diagonal lies inside the polygon.

Suppose that P_{i-1}, P_i, P_{i+1} are three successive vertices, where we define $P_{-1} = P_{n-1}$ and $P_n = P_0$, to allow the cases $i = 0$ and $i = n - 1$. Remember that the vertices are given in counter-clockwise order. Then P_i is a convex vertex if and only if the three vertices P_{i-1}, P_i, P_{i+1}, in that order, are also traversed counter-clockwise. As a counter-example, consider Fig. 3.10, where triple $P_1P_2P_3$ is clockwise, P_2 is non-convex and diagonal P_1P_3 lies outside the polygon. Thus diagonal $P_{i-1}P_{i+1}$ can only be a candidate for our purposes if $P_{i-1}(x_{i-1}, y_{i-1})$, $P_i(x_i, y_i)$, $P_{i+1}(x_{i+1}, y_{i+1})$, in that order, are traversed counter-clockwise, that is, if

$$D = \begin{vmatrix} x_{i-1} & y_{i-1} & 1 \\ x_i & y_i & 1 \\ x_{i+1} & y_{i+1} & 1 \end{vmatrix} > 0$$

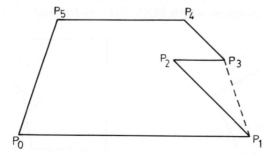

Fig. 3.10. Diagonal P_1P_3 outside polygon

[1] We shall use a method which works properly for a large class of polygons. However, there are polygons for which the method will fail, see Exercise 3-3 at the end of this chapter.

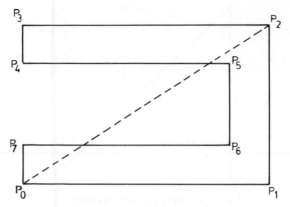

Fig. 3.11. Diagonal $P_0 P_2$ partly outside polygon

This condition is necessary, but, unfortunately, it is not sufficient, as is shown by Fig. 3.11. Here P_0, P_1, P_2, in that order, are traversed counter-clockwise yet $P_0 P_2$ cannot be used to divide the polygon into triangles. This situation can be avoided by taking the lengths of the diagonals into account. We shall choose the shortest diagonal $P_{i-1} P_{i+1}$ that has a convex vertex P_i between P_{i-1} and P_{i+1}. This diagonal is used to cut off triangle $P_{i-1} P_i P_{i+1}$. Then the remaining polygon

$$P_0, P_1, \ldots, P_{i-1}, P_{i+1}, \ldots, P_{n-1}$$

is treated in the same way, and so on. Technically this is realized by introducing an integer array $v_0, \ldots, v_{m-1}$, containing the vertex numbers of the remaining polygon. Initially we set $m = n$ and $v_i = i$ ($i = 0, 1, \ldots, n-1$). Every time a triangle is cut off, m is decremented. If a program like this is meant for practical use many tests on the validity of the input data are desirable. A program that adequately rejects any set of invalid input data is said to be *robust*. In our situation, it makes sense to test whether the given input sequence

$$n \quad x_0 \ y_0 \quad x_1 \ y_1 \ \ldots \ x_{n-1} \ y_{n-1}$$

describe a polygon at all. This is not the case with the sequence

$$4 \quad 1 \ 1 \quad 2 \ 2 \quad 2 \ 1 \quad 1 \ 2$$

since traversing the points in the given order will yield Fig. 3.12, which we do not accept as a polygon.

Other tests that are appropriate concern

The maximum value of n, e.g. $n \leq 500$;
The minimum and maximum value of the co-ordinates;
The required counter-clockwise orientation.

Despite their importance, most of these tests have been omitted here and left as an exercise for the reader. On the other hand, the program will contain a special feature, which, strictly speaking, could also have been omitted, namely the representation of diagonals by dashed lines instead of by unbroken lines. We shall

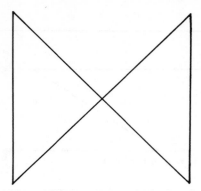

Fig. 3.12. Result of invalid sequence

require all dashes of a dashed line to have the same length. A dashed line must not start or end with a gap, but there should be a full dash at the beginning and at the end of the dashed line, as shown for segment PQ in Fig. 3.13.

P ▬▬ ▬▬ ▬▬ ▬▬ ▬▬ ▬▬ ▬▬ Q

Fig. 3.13. A dashed line

The reader is encouraged to solve this problem and to compare his solution with the function *dash* in the following program.

```
/* POLY_TRIA:   Dividing a polygon into triangles */
#define NMAX 500
#define BIG 1.0e30
#include <math.h>
int n, v[NMAX]; float x[NMAX], y[NMAX];

main()
{ int i, h, j, m, l, imin;
  double diag, min_diag;
  printf("%s\n%s\n",
  "Give n, followed by n coordinate pairs (x, y) of the vertices, ",
  "in counter-clockwise order");
  scanf("%d", &n); if (n>=NMAX) { printf("n too large"); exit(1); }
  for (i=0; i<n; i++) { scanf("%f %f", &x[i], &y[i]); v[i]=i; }
  initgr(); draw_polygon(); m=n;
  while (m>3)
  { min_diag=BIG;
    for (i=0; i<m; i++)
    { h= (i==0 ? m-1 : i-1); j= (i==m-1 ? 0 : i+1);
      if (counter_clock(h, i, j, &diag) && diag<min_diag)
      { min_diag=diag; imin=i;
      }
    }
    i=imin; h= (i==0 ? m-1 : i-1); j= (i==m-1 ? 0 : i+1);
    if (min_diag==BIG) error("wrong sense of rotation");
    dash(x[v[h]], y[v[h]], x[v[j]], y[v[j]]);
    m--;
    for (l=i; l<m; l++) v[l]=v[l+1];
  }
```

```
  endgr();
}

error(str) char *str;
{ endgr(); printf("%s\n", str); exit(1);
}

int counter_clock(h, i, j, pdist) int h, i, j; double *pdist;
{ double xh=x[v[h]], xi=x[v[i]], xj=x[v[j]],
         yh=y[v[h]], yi=y[v[i]], yj=y[v[j]],
         x_hi, y_hi, x_hj, y_hj, Determ;
  x_hi=xi-xh; y_hi=yi-yh;  x_hj=xj-xh; y_hj=yj-yh;
  *pdist = x_hj * x_hj + y_hj * y_hj;
  Determ = x_hi * y_hj - x_hj * y_hi;
  return Determ>1e-6;
}

draw_polygon()
{ int i;
  move(x[n-1], y[n-1]);
  for (i=0; i<n; i++) draw(x[i], y[i]);
}

dash(x1, y1, x2, y2) float x1, y1, x2, y2;
{ int i, k;
  float xdif=x2-x1, ydif=y2-y1, pitch0=0.3, dx, dy;
  k = 2 * (int) ceil(sqrt(xdif*xdif+ydif*ydif)/pitch0) + 1;
  dx=xdif/k; dy=ydif/k;
  for (i=0; i<k; i+=2)
  { move(x1+i*dx, y1+i*dy); draw(x1+(i+1)*dx, y1+(i+1)*dy);
  }
}
```

The following input sequence

```
          12
       1 1  6 1  6 4  4 4  4 3  5 3
       5 2  2 2  2 3  3 3  3 4  1 4
```

will lead to Fig. 3.14 as output.

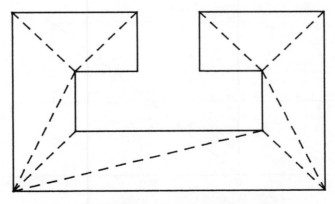

Fig. 3.14. Output of program POLY_TRIA

3.6 HOMOGENEOUS CO-ORDINATES

This section deals with a mathematically interesting topic which is related to perspective and therefore often included in books on three-dimensional computer graphics. We shall conform to this usage in order to obtain a better understanding of notations such as $[x \quad y \quad 1]$ and $[x \quad y \quad z \quad 1]$. This section deals with geometry, and though not particularly difficult, it is rather long and theoretical. Readers who are interested primarily in practical aspects of graphics programming might skip to Section 3.7 without serious consequences for the study of the rest of the book. They can return to this point at a later stage.

In Section 2.3 we used the notation $[x \quad y \quad 1]$ to denote a matrix of only one row, sometimes called a row vector. This notation could also have been introduced as a special case of $[x \quad y \quad w]$ where x, y, w are called *homogeneous co-ordinates*. We use three homogeneous co-ordinates to denote a point in two-dimensional space (2-space, for short). In projective geometry homogeneous co-ordinates had been used long before computer graphics became popular. In Chapter 4 we shall deal with perspective transformations. They are in fact central projections, treated thoroughly in books on projective geometry. We shall briefly discuss only a few of the topics of this fascinating but rather difficult branch of mathematics, avoiding formal definitions and rigorously proven theorems.

In Fig. 3.15 we have an x-axis and a w-axis, so a point is given by its co-ordinate pair (x, w). Any point $P(x, w)$ not on the x-axis has its central projection $P'(X, 1)$, being the intersection of line OP and line l with equation $w = 1$. The origin O is the centre of projection. Line segment PO can be considered as a ray of light from an object P to the eye O. Introducing the points $Q(0, w)$ and $Q'(0, 1)$, we have two similar triangles OPQ and OP'Q', so that

$$X = \frac{X}{1} = \frac{P'Q'}{OQ'} = \frac{PQ}{OQ} = \frac{x}{w}$$

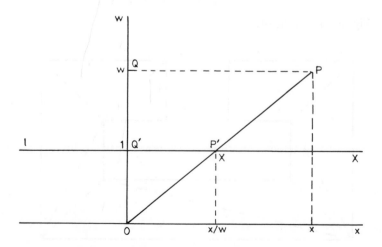

Fig. 3.15. Two-dimensional central projection

All points (x, w) with the property $x = wX$ lie on line OP and have the same projection P′. If we are interested only in projections on line l, not the actual values x and w but only their ratio matters. It is natural to use only one co-ordinate X instead of a co-ordinate pair $(X, 1)$ if we deal only with points on line l. Should we insist on using a co-ordinate pair, any number pair (x, w) satisfying $x/w = X$ would do if we so agreed. In geometric terms the co-ordinate pair (wX, w) of any point P, distinct from O, on line OP′ could serve as a notation for point P′. This is what is done when homogeneous co-ordinates are used. In general, any point $(X_1, X_2, \ldots, X_n)$ in n-space is written as a point $(wX_1, wX_2, \ldots, wX_n, w)$ in $(n + 1)$-space, where w is any non-zero real number. The latter $n + 1$ numbers are said to be homogeneous co-ordinates of the original point in n-space. The reader will probably be familiar with the notion of projection, being a many-to-one mapping from $(n + 1)$-space to n-space. Homogeneous co-ordinates arise from the reverse process, a one-to-many mapping from n-space to $(n + 1)$-space. Point $(5, 7)$ in 2-space, for example, can be written in homogeneous co-ordinates as $(15, 21, 3)$, or as $(500, 700, 100)$, etc. Though mainly interested in 2-space, we can consider these triples as points in 3-space. Obviously, (X, Y) is the usual 2-space notation for point $(X, Y, 1)$ in 3-space. This point, P′, is the central projection of any point $P(x, y, w)$, if $x/w = X$ and $y/w = Y$. Again the origin O is the centre of projection; all point are now projected to the plane $w = 1$.

To explain the term *homogeneous* let us consider the equation

$$aX + bY + c = 0 \tag{3.6}$$

representing a line in 2-space. Replacing X and Y with x/w and y/w, we have

$$a(x/w) + b(y/w) + c = 0$$

or
$$ax + by + cw = 0 \tag{3.7}$$

It is customary to call Eq. (3.7) homogeneous, because of the identical structure of the terms ax, by, cw. It is therefore reasonable to call x, y, w homogeneous co-ordinates of point (X, Y). If the 2-space is again the plane $w = 1$ in an xyw-co-ordinate system, then Eq. (3.7) is the plane through the origin O and the given line.

If (x, y, w) were merely used as another notation for $(x/w, y/w)$ it would be necessary to stipulate that w be non-zero. However, in this way homogeneous co-ordinates would hardly have any advantages over conventional ones, and the reader will probably wonder whether they have any at all. To do them justice, we have to admit that $w = 0$, as we shall see presently. Homogeneous co-ordinates lead to elegant and general formulations of geometrical properties. For example, let us consider a system of two linear equations, each representing a line in 2-space:

$$\begin{cases} a_1X + b_1Y + c_1 = 0 \\ a_2X + b_2Y + c_2 = 0 \end{cases} \tag{3.8}$$

If the two lines are parallel, they have no point of intersection and there is no number pair (X, Y) satisfying Eqs (3.8). Thus to find a common point of the two lines we have to use a rule with an exception, which is not particularly elegant. Replacing X and Y with the homogeneous co-ordinates x, y, w will improve the situation:

$$\begin{cases} a_1x + b_1y + c_1w = 0 \\ a_2x + b_2y + c_2w = 0 \end{cases} \tag{3.9}$$

Equations (3.9) can also be interpreted as planes through O; they have at least the trivial solution $x = y = w = 0$. For a geometrical interpretation we choose concrete values for the coefficients. Let us, for example, replace Eqs (3.8) with

$$\begin{cases} 2X + 3Y - 6 = 0 \\ 4X + 6Y - 24 = 0 \end{cases}$$

representing the parallel lines of Fig. 3.16. We then have to replace Eqs (3.9) with

$$\begin{cases} 2x + 3y - 6w = 0 \tag{3.10a} \\ 4x + 6y - 24w = 0 \tag{3.10b} \end{cases}$$

This system is equivalent to

$$\begin{cases} 2x + 3y = 0 \\ w = 0 \end{cases}$$

so the solution consists of all triples $(3k, -2k, 0)$, where k is any real number. In 3-space these points constitute the line through O and $(3, -2, 0)$, this line being the intersection of the planes given by Eqs (3.10a, b). Returning to the 2-space of the plane $w = 1$, we remember that every point (X, Y) is associated with the line (wX, wY, w) in 3-space. For non-zero w-values this association is almost trivial. An important motivation for the use of homogeneous co-ordinates will now become

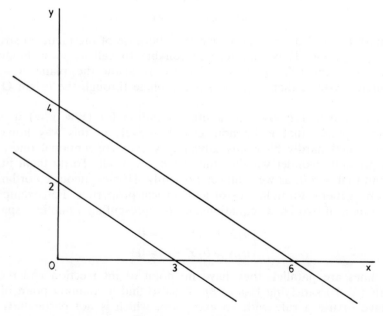

Fig. 3.16. Parallel lines

clear. To every line in 2-space we add an object called *infinite point*. This infinite point cannot be written in conventional co-ordinates, but it can in homogeneous co-ordinates. For example, the infinite point of the line of Eq. (3.10a) is written as $(3, -2, 0)$ or as any other triple $(3k, -2k, 0)$ with non-zero k. Since these triples are solutions to both Eqs (3.10a) and (3.10b) this infinite point is said to be the intersection of the two parallel lines in Fig. 3.16. Note that this infinite point of intersection is considered to be a point in 2-space. As we have seen, every point in 2-space is associated with a line in 3-space, so we might wonder what line the infinite point $(3, -2, 0)$ is associated with. Since this has to be the line through the given point and $O(0, 0, 0)$, the line we looked for is the one through O and $(3, -2, 0)$, lying in the plane $w = 0$.

It is reasonable to call $(3, -2, 0)$ an infinite point, since we can regard it as the limit of $(3, -2, w)$ where w goes to 0, and the latter triple in homogeneous co-ordinates is equivalent to $(3/w, -2/w, 1)$ which lies far away for small values of w. The notion of infinite points enables us to say that any two distinct lines in 2-space meet in one point. In the same way we say in projective geometry that any two distinct planes in 3-space have a line of intersection. If the planes are parallel, all points on this line of intersection are written $(x, y, z, 0)$ in homogeneous co-ordinates. We shall not discuss this in greater detail, but return to 2-space and show other new possibilities offered by homogeneous co-ordinates.

With non-homogeneous co-ordinates a linear transformation in 2-space can be written

$$[X' \quad Y'] = [X \quad Y]A$$
$$A = \begin{bmatrix} a_1 & a_2 \\ b_1 & b_2 \end{bmatrix}$$

Since $[1 \quad 0]A = [a_1 \quad a_2]$ and $[0 \quad 1]A = [b_1 \quad b_2]$, the rows of matrix A are the images of $[1 \quad 0]$ and $[0 \quad 1]$, respectively.

No matter how A is defined, the origin O is self-corresponding, that is, $[0 \quad 0]A = [0 \quad 0]$, so a translation cannot be expressed in this way. In homogeneous co-ordinates, however, a point in 2-space is given by a triple (x, y, w) and a transformation is written

$$[x' \quad y' \quad w'] = [x \quad y \quad w]A$$
$$A = \begin{bmatrix} a_1 & a_2 & a_3 \\ b_1 & b_2 & b_3 \\ c_1 & c_2 & c_3 \end{bmatrix}$$

We have

$$[1 \quad 0 \quad 0]A = [a_1 \quad a_2 \quad a_3]$$

Point $[1 \quad 0 \quad 0]$ is the infinite point of the x-axis. Thus the first row $[a_1 \quad a_2 \quad a_3]$ of matrix A is the image of the infinite point of the x-axis. Similarly, the second row $[b_1 \quad b_2 \quad b_3]$ is the image of the infinite point of the y-axis. Since

$$[0 \quad 0 \quad 1]A = [c_1 \quad c_2 \quad c_3]$$

we see that the third row $[c_1 \quad c_2 \quad c_3]$ is the image of the origin $[0 \quad 0 \quad 1]$. This

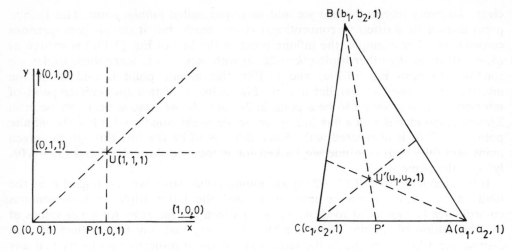

Fig. 3.17. Quadrant mapped into a triangle

means that homogeneous co-ordinates enable us to express any translation by a matrix multiplication. In fact this is nothing new, since we already used it in Section 2.3. However, translation is not the only new possibility offered by this type of matrix multiplication; we can also map parallel lines to intersecting lines. We shall show this, mapping a complete rectangular quadrant to a triangle.

In Fig. 3.17 we have an arbitrary triangle whose vertices are in rectangular co-ordinates $A(a_1, a_2)$, $B(b_1, b_2)$, $C(c_1, c_2)$. We have added a third co-ordinate 1 as a formal means of obtaining homogeneous co-ordinates. Exceptions are the infinite points $(1, 0, 0)$ and $(0, 1, 0)$ of the co-ordinates axes, whose third homogeneous co-ordinates are zero. We shall now construct a matrix M, such that the matrix multiplication

$$[x' \quad y' \quad z'] = [x \quad y \quad z]M$$

maps point O to C, point $(1, 0, 0)$ to A and point $(0, 1, 0)$ to B. For any non-zero values α, β, γ the points A, B, C will be the required image points if

$$M = \begin{bmatrix} \alpha a_1 & \alpha a_2 & \alpha \\ \beta b_1 & \beta b_2 & \beta \\ \gamma c_1 & \gamma c_2 & \gamma \end{bmatrix} \tag{3.8}$$

This is easily verified, since we have, for example,

$$[1 \quad 0 \quad 0]M = [\alpha a_1 \quad \alpha a_2 \quad \alpha]$$

whose right-hand side is just another notation for point A in Fig. 3.17. At first sight it seems that the constants α, β, γ in Eq. (3.8) are not relevant and can be set to 1. We need them, however, to be able to prescribe the image U' of the so-called unit point U. Point U' may be chosen anywhere inside triangle ABC. Since $U(1, 1, 1)$ maps to $U'(u_1, u_2, 1)$, we have

$$[1 \quad 1 \quad 1]M = [u_1 \quad u_2 \quad 1]$$

which is short-hand for the following system of three linear equations in α, β, γ:

$$a_1\alpha + b_1\beta + c_1\gamma = u_1$$
$$a_2\alpha + b_2\beta + c_2\gamma = u_2$$
$$\alpha + \beta + \gamma = 1$$

This system has a unique solution, which follows from the fact that $(a_1, a_2, 1)$, $(b_1, b_2, 1)$, $(c_1, c_2, 1)$ denote vertices of a triangle. Solving this system for α, β, γ and substituting the results into Eq. (3.8) gives us the desired matrix M.

Straight lines map to straight lines, but parallelism is not preserved. For example, the vertical line through point U in Fig. 3.17 maps to the line through B and U'. This provides a geometrical means to find the projection P' of point P. Having computed matrix M we can find P' analytically as the product

$$[1 \quad 0 \quad 1]M$$

Note that every infinite point maps to a point on AB, and that the infinite points of parallel lines map to a single point on AB. It makes sense to view the entire quadrant as a flat landscape of which triangle ABC is a picture and AB is the horizon.

This concludes our discussion on homogeneous co-ordinates. For many more interesting properties the reader is referred to a textbook on projective geometry such as Hopkins and Hails (1953).

3.7 THREE-DIMENSIONAL TRANSLATIONS AND ROTATIONS

If every point P(x, y, z) is mapped to a point P'(x', y', z'), according to

$$\begin{cases} x' = x + a_1 \\ y' = y + a_2 \\ z' = z + a_3 \end{cases}$$

where a_1, a_2, a_3 are constants, we have a translation in three-dimensional space. This translation can also be written

$$[x' \quad y' \quad z' \quad 1] = [x \quad y \quad z \quad 1]T$$

$$T = \begin{bmatrix} 1 & 0 & 0 & 0 \\ 0 & 1 & 0 & 0 \\ 0 & 0 & 1 & 0 \\ a_1 & a_2 & a_3 & 1 \end{bmatrix} \tag{3.9}$$

Readers who have studied Section 3.6 will know that the first, the second and the third rows of matrix T denote (images of) the infinite points of the co-ordinate axes, and that the fourth row is the image of $[0 \quad 0 \quad 0 \quad 1]$. The latter means that in homogeneous co-ordinates $[a_1 \quad a_2 \quad a_3 \quad 1]$ is the image of the origin 0.

Rotations about the co-ordinate axes can be expressed with matrices without using homogeneous co-ordinates. For the sake of brevity we shall do so now and switch to homogeneous co-ordinates when we actually need them. We use a right-handed co-ordinate system, and we call a rotation about an axis positive if it

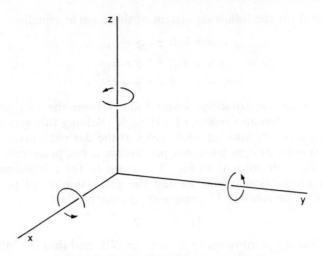

Fig. 3.18. Positive rotations about axes

corresponds to the positive direction of that axis in the sense of a right-handed screw. This is shown in Fig. 3.18.

We shall rotate about the z-axis through an angle α, and abbreviate $\cos \alpha = c$, $\sin \alpha = s$. The rotation is then written:

$$[x' \quad y' \quad z'] = [x \quad y \quad z]R_z$$

$$R_z = \begin{bmatrix} c & s & 0 \\ -s & c & 0 \\ 0 & 0 & 1 \end{bmatrix}$$

which follows from Section 2.3, Eq. (2.4).

This matrix R_z can be used to derive the matrices R_x and R_y for rotations about the other two axes in a formal way, that is, without using a picture. This is done by the cyclic permutation obtained by replacing each of the letters x, y, z with its successor, the successor of z being x.

We convert R_z into R_x by cyclic advancing each row one position, followed by a similar operation on the columns:

$$R_z = \begin{bmatrix} c & s & 0 \\ -s & c & 0 \\ 0 & 0 & 1 \end{bmatrix} \quad \begin{bmatrix} 0 & 0 & 1 \\ c & s & 0 \\ -s & c & 0 \end{bmatrix}$$

$$\begin{bmatrix} 1 & 0 & 0 \\ 0 & c & s \\ 0 & -s & c \end{bmatrix} = R_x$$

In the same way R_x is converted into its 'successor' R_y:

$$R_x = \begin{bmatrix} 1 & 0 & 0 \\ 0 & c & s \\ 0 & -s & c \end{bmatrix} \quad \begin{bmatrix} 0 & -s & c \\ 1 & 0 & 0 \\ 0 & c & s \end{bmatrix}$$

$$\begin{bmatrix} c & 0 & -s \\ 0 & 1 & 0 \\ s & 0 & c \end{bmatrix} = R_y$$

Summarizing, we have the following matrices:

$$R_x = \begin{bmatrix} 1 & 0 & 0 \\ 0 & \cos \alpha & \sin \alpha \\ 0 & -\sin \alpha & \cos \alpha \end{bmatrix} \tag{3.10}$$

$$R_y = \begin{bmatrix} \cos \alpha & 0 & -\sin \alpha \\ 0 & 1 & 0 \\ \sin \alpha & 0 & \cos \alpha \end{bmatrix} \tag{3.11}$$

$$R_z = \begin{bmatrix} \cos \alpha & \sin \alpha & 0 \\ -\sin \alpha & \cos \alpha & 0 \\ 0 & 0 & 1 \end{bmatrix} \tag{3.12}$$

Matrix R_x is used in the following way:

$$[x' \quad y' \quad z'] = [x \quad y \quad z]R_x$$

for a rotation about the x-axis through an angle α, and the matrices R_y and R_z are used similarly.

As explained in Section 2.1, equations for a transformation can also be interpreted as a change of co-ordinates. Moving a point a certain distance to the right requires the same equations as moving the co-ordinate system the same distance to the left. In practice it is more convenient to move the co-ordinate system in the same sense as points would have been moved, but this requires inverted matrices. Fortunately, the inverses of T, R_x, R_y, R_z (Eqs (3.9)–(3.12)) can be written down immediately:

$$T^{-1} = \begin{bmatrix} 1 & 0 & 0 & 0 \\ 0 & 1 & 0 & 0 \\ 0 & 0 & 1 & 0 \\ -a_1 & -a_2 & -a_3 & 1 \end{bmatrix} \tag{3.13}$$

$$R_x^{-1} = \begin{bmatrix} 1 & 0 & 0 \\ 0 & \cos \alpha & -\sin \alpha \\ 0 & \sin \alpha & \cos \alpha \end{bmatrix} \tag{3.14}$$

$$R_y^{-1} = \begin{bmatrix} \cos \alpha & 0 & \sin \alpha \\ 0 & 1 & 0 \\ -\sin \alpha & 0 & \cos \alpha \end{bmatrix} \qquad (3.15)$$

$$R_z^{-1} = \begin{bmatrix} \cos \alpha & -\sin \alpha & 0 \\ \sin \alpha & \cos \alpha & 0 \\ 0 & 0 & 1 \end{bmatrix} \qquad (3.16)$$

We are now in a position to find the matrix R for a rotation about any line passing through the origin O. To define the sense of rotation we prefer to say that we rotate about a vector $\mathbf{v}$ whose initial point is O. Then a positive rotation corresponds to the vector direction according to a right-handed screw. As before, we shall rotate through an angle α.

If the endpoint of $\mathbf{v}$ is given in rectangular co-ordinates we first compute its spherical co-ordinates ρ, θ, φ (see Fig. 3.19):

$$\rho = |\mathbf{v}| = \sqrt{(v_1^2 + v_2^2 + v_3^2)}$$

If $\rho = 0$, we set $\theta = \varphi = 0$. Otherwise

$$\theta = \begin{cases} \arctan (v_2/v_1) & \text{if} \quad v_1 > 0 \\ \pi + \arctan (v_2/v_1) & \text{if} \quad v_1 < 0 \\ \pi/2 & \text{if} \quad v_1 = 0 \quad \text{and} \quad v_2 \geqslant 0 \\ 3\pi/2 & \text{if} \quad v_1 = 0 \quad \text{and} \quad v_2 < 0 \end{cases}$$

$$\varphi = \arccos (v_3/\rho)$$

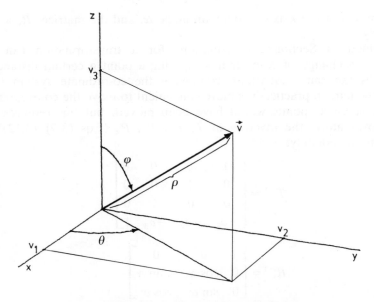

Fig. 3.19. Spherical co-ordinates

(The reader will probably be more familiar with the reverse computation:

$$v_1 = \rho \sin \varphi \cos \theta, \qquad v_2 = \rho \sin \varphi \sin \theta, \qquad v_3 = \rho \cos \varphi)$$

Our strategy will now be to change the co-ordinate system such that $\mathbf{v}$, the axis of rotation, will lie on the new positive z-axis. We begin with a rotation of the x- and y-axes about the z-axis through an angle θ. According to Eq. (3.16) we can write this as

$$[x' \quad y' \quad z'] = [x \quad y \quad z]R_z^{-1}$$

$$R_z^{-1} = \begin{bmatrix} \cos \theta & -\sin \theta & 0 \\ \sin \theta & \cos \theta & 0 \\ 0 & 0 & 1 \end{bmatrix}$$

The x'-axis has the positive direction of vector $(v_1 \, v_2 \, 0)$. Then we rotate the x'- and the z'-axes about the y'-axis through an angle φ, yielding a z"-axis in the direction of vector $\mathbf{v}$ (see Fig. 3.19).

Referring to Eq. (3.15) we write this as

$$[x'' \quad y'' \quad z''] = [x' \quad x' \quad z']R_y^{-1}$$

$$R_y^{-1} = \begin{bmatrix} \cos \varphi & 0 & \sin \varphi \\ 0 & 1 & 0 \\ -\sin \varphi & 0 & \cos \varphi \end{bmatrix}$$

The actual rotation about $\mathbf{v}$ through an angle α can now be performed as a rotation about the z"-axis. Referring to Eq. (3.12) we have

$$[x''' \quad y''' \quad z'''] = [x'' \quad y'' \quad z'']R_v$$

$$R_v = \begin{bmatrix} \cos \alpha & \sin \alpha & 0 \\ -\sin \alpha & \cos \alpha & 0 \\ 0 & 0 & 1 \end{bmatrix}$$

So far, we have achieved the following:

$$[x''' \quad y''' \quad z'''] = [x \quad y \quad z]R_z^{-1}R_y^{-1}R_v$$

Unfortunately, the co-ordinates x''', y''', z''' refer to the latest co-ordinate system, whereas we want them expressed as the original co-ordinates. We shall denote these original co-ordinates of the rotated point by x^*, y^*, z^*. Reverting to the original co-ordinates is accomplished by applying the inverses of matrices R_z^{-1} and R_y^{-1} (being R_z and R_y) in reverse order to x''', y''', z''':

$$[x^* \quad y^* \quad z^*] = [x''' \quad y''' \quad z''']R_yR_z$$

This means that the complete rotation about vector $\mathbf{v}$ through the angle α is computed as follows:

$$[x^* \quad y^* \quad z^*] = [x \quad y \quad z]R_z^{-1}R_y^{-1}R_vR_yR_z$$

where

$$R_z^{-1} = \begin{bmatrix} \cos\theta & -\sin\theta & 0 \\ \sin\theta & \cos\theta & 0 \\ 0 & 0 & 1 \end{bmatrix}$$

$$R_y^{-1} = \begin{bmatrix} \cos\varphi & 0 & \sin\varphi \\ 0 & 1 & 0 \\ -\sin\varphi & 0 & \cos\varphi \end{bmatrix}$$

$$R_v = \begin{bmatrix} \cos\alpha & \sin\alpha & 0 \\ -\sin\alpha & \cos\alpha & 0 \\ 0 & 0 & 1 \end{bmatrix}$$

$$R_y = \begin{bmatrix} \cos\varphi & 0 & -\sin\varphi \\ 0 & 1 & 0 \\ \sin\varphi & 0 & \cos\varphi \end{bmatrix}$$

$$R_z = \begin{bmatrix} \cos\theta & \sin\theta & 0 \\ -\sin\theta & \cos\theta & 0 \\ 0 & 0 & 1 \end{bmatrix}$$

For later purposes, let us write

$$R_z^{-1}R_y^{-1}R_vR_yR_z = R = \begin{bmatrix} r_{11} & r_{12} & r_{13} \\ r_{21} & r_{22} & r_{23} \\ r_{31} & r_{32} & r_{33} \end{bmatrix} \tag{3.17}$$

Up to now we have discussed rotations about vectors with origin O as their initial point. We now wish to drop the latter restriction and to perform a rotation about a vector $\mathbf{v}$ whose initial point can be any given point $A(a_1, a_2, a_3)$. To achieve this, we use vector $\mathbf{v}$ to compute matrix R of Eq. (3.17) in the same way as before. The following three steps are then taken:

(1) Referring to Eq. (3.13), we perform a translation from the given point A to the origin O, using homogeneous co-ordinates and the following matrix:

$$T^{-1} = \begin{bmatrix} 1 & 0 & 0 & 0 \\ 0 & 1 & 0 & 0 \\ 0 & 0 & 1 & 0 \\ -a_1 & -a_2 & -a_3 & 1 \end{bmatrix}$$

(2) We can now rotate about an axis passing through O as before, but we extend matrix R of Eq. (3.17) in a trivial way to be able to apply it to homogeneous co-ordinates:

$$R^* = \begin{bmatrix} r_{11} & r_{12} & r_{13} & 0 \\ r_{21} & r_{22} & r_{23} & 0 \\ r_{31} & r_{32} & r_{33} & 0 \\ 0 & 0 & 0 & 1 \end{bmatrix}$$

(3) We apply a translation opposite to that in (1) using:

$$T = \begin{bmatrix} 1 & 0 & 0 & 0 \\ 0 & 1 & 0 & 0 \\ 0 & 0 & 1 & 0 \\ a_1 & a_2 & a_3 & 1 \end{bmatrix}$$

The general rotation matrix is then

$$R_{\text{GEN}} = T^{-1} R^* T$$

and it is used as follows:

$$[x^* \quad y^* \quad z^* \quad 1] = [x \quad y \quad z \quad 1] R_{\text{GEN}}$$

EXERCISES

3.1 Investigate the effect of choosing $\alpha = \beta = \gamma = 1$ in Section 3.6, Eq. (3.8) and write a program to perform the mapping from the quadrant to a given triangle for some points. Produce the triangle and the images of $(1, 1)$, $(1, 2)$, $(1, 3), \ldots$; $(2, 1)$, $(2, 2)$, $(2, 3), \ldots$, etc. in graphical form.

3.2 Write a program for a general rotation. The input of the program will be:

(1) The co-ordinates of two points A and B, determining the vector $\mathbf{v} = \mathbf{AB}$ with initial point A.

(2) The angle α. The rotation will then take place about vector $\mathbf{v}$ and through angle α.

(3) A set of points to be rotated.

The output of the program has to be the rotated points. Each point is expressed as a triple of rectangular co-ordinates. Since we have not yet dealt with graphical output of three-dimensional objects produce the output in numerical form.

3.3 Find a polygon that will not be dealt with correctly by program *POLY_TRIA*, and develop a more general algorithm.

Hint: If a triangle is cut off a polygon, none of the other vertices may lie inside that triangle.

CHAPTER 4

Perspective

4.1 INTRODUCTION

In Fig. 4.1 a two-dimensional representation of a cube is shown along with some auxiliary lines. In this picture lines such as AB and AD are not parallel to the lower and upper edges of the paper, so one could argue that they are not horizontal. However, they denote horizontal edges of the cube ABCDEFGH in three-dimensional space and we shall therefore briefly call them horizontal lines. For the same reason we shall say that two lines such as AB and DC are parallel, implicitly thinking in three dimensions. In this terminology, parallel horizontal lines meet in a so-called *vanishing point*. All these vanishing points lie on the same line, which is called the *horizon*. Note that the horizon and vanishing points are picture concepts, not really existing in three-dimensional space. For many centuries these concepts have been used by artists to draw realistic pictures of three-dimensional objects and it is customary to call such pictures perspective.

The invention of photography offered a new (and easier) way of producing perspective pictures. There is a strong analogy between a camera used in photography and the human eye. Our eye is a very sophisticated instrument of which a camera is an imitation. In the following discussion the word *eye* may be replaced with *camera* if we wish to emphasize that two-dimensional hard copy is wanted.

It is obvious that the picture will depend on the position of the eye. An important aspect is the distance between the eye and the object, since the 'perspective effect' will be inversely proportional to this distance. If the eye is close to the object we have a strong perspective effect as in Fig. 4.2(a). Here we can very clearly see that in the picture the extensions of parallel line segments will meet. On the other hand, if the eye is very far from the object (compared with the size of the object), parallel lines seem to be parallel in the picture. This is shown in Fig. 4.2(b).

Besides the classical and the photographical methods there is a way of producing perspective pictures which is based on analytical geometry. We are by now very familiar with representing points in 2-space and 3-space by their co-ordinates (X, Y) and (x, y, z), respectively. (Again we write 'n-space' as short-hand for 'n-dimensional space'.) If we wish to produce a perspective drawing we are given a great many points $P(x, y, z)$ of the object and we want their images $P'(X, Y)$ in the picture. Thus all we need is a mapping from the so-called *world co-ordinates* (x, y, z) of a point P to the *screen co-ordinates* (X, Y) of its central projection P'. We imagine a screen between the object and the eye E. For every point P of the object the line PE intersects the screen in point P'. It is convenient to perform this mapping in two stages. The first is called *viewing transformation*; point P is left at its place but we change from world co-ordinates to so-called *eye co-ordinates*. The

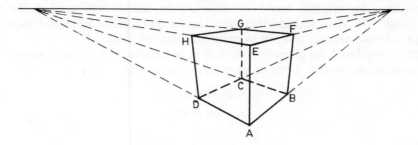

Fig. 4.1. Vanishing points at the horizon

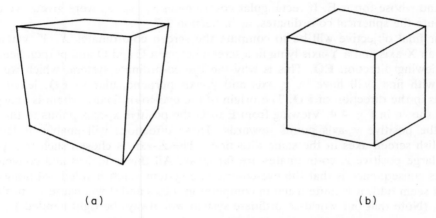

(a)   (b)

Fig. 4.2. (a) *Eye close to object*; (b) *eye far from object*

second stage is called *perspective transformation*. This is a proper transformation from P to P′, combined with a transition from the three-dimensional eye co-ordinates to the two-dimensional screen co-ordinates:

World co-ordinates (x_w, y_w, z_w)

Viewing transformation ↓

Eye co-ordinates (x_e, y_e, z_e)

Perspective transformation ↓

Screen co-ordinates (X, Y)

4.2 THE VIEWING TRANSFORMATION

To perform the viewing transformation the viewpoint E, being the position of the eye, and an object must be given. Let us require that the world-co-ordinate system be right-handed. It is convenient if it has its origin O lying more or less central in the object, since we then view the object from E to O. We shall assume that this is the case; in practice this might require a co-ordinate transformation consisting of decrementing the original world co-ordinates by the co-ordinates of the central object point. We shall include this very simple co-ordinate transformation in our program, without writing it down in mathematical notation.

Let the viewpoint E be given in spherical co-ordinates ρ, θ, φ, with respect to the world-co-ordinate system. Thus its world co-ordinates are

$$x_E = \rho \sin \varphi \cos \theta$$
$$y_E = \rho \sin \varphi \sin \theta \qquad\qquad (4.1)$$
$$z_E = \rho \cos \varphi$$

as shown in Fig. 4.3. The direction of vector **EO** ($= -$**OE**) is said to be the viewing direction. From our eye in E we can only see points within some cone whose axis is EO and whose top is E. If rectangular co-ordinates x_E, y_E, z_E were given, we could compute the spherical co-ordinates, as in Section 3.7.

Our final objective will be to compute the screen co-ordinates X, Y, where we have an X-axis and a Y-axis lying in a screen between E and O and perpendicular to the viewing direction **EO**. This is why the eye-co-ordinate system, which we shall deal with first, will have its x_e-axis and y_e-axis perpendicular to **EO**, leaving the z_e-axis in the direction of **EO**. The origin of the eye-co-ordinate system is viewpoint E, as shown in Fig. 4.4. Viewing from E to O the positive x_e-axis points to the right and the positive y_e-axis points upwards. These directions will enable us later to establish screen axes in the same directions. The z_e-axis is chosen such that points with large positive z_e-co-ordinates are far away. All this is logical and convenient, but its consequence is that the eye-co-ordinate system is left-handed. Although this might seem odd, it is quite usual in computer graphics and it will cause no problems at all. (Note that our world-co-ordinate system will always be right-handed.)

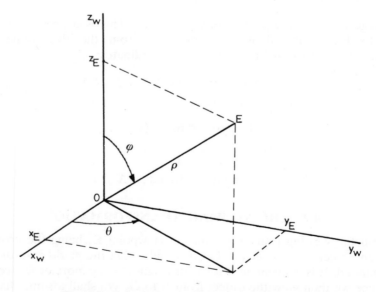

Fig. 4.3. Spherical co-ordinates of viewpoint E

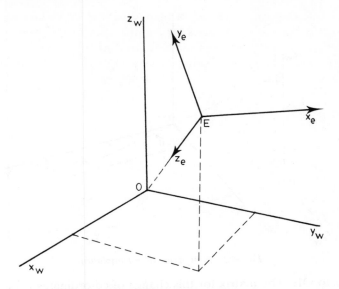

Fig. 4.4. Eye-co-ordinate system

The viewing transformation can be written

$$[x_e \quad y_e \quad z_e \quad 1] = [x_w \quad y_w \quad z_w \quad 1]V \qquad (4.2)$$

where V is the 4×4 viewing matrix. To find V we imagine the viewing transformation to be composed of four elementary transformations, for which the matrices can easily be written down. Matrix V will be the product of these four matrices. Each of the four transformations is in fact a change of co-ordinates and has therefore a matrix which is the inverse of the matrix that a similar point transformation would have.

(1) Moving the origin from O to E

We perform a translation of the co-ordinate system such that viewpoint E becomes the new origin. The matrix for this change of co-ordinates is:

$$T = \begin{bmatrix} 1 & 0 & 0 & 0 \\ 0 & 1 & 0 & 0 \\ 0 & 0 & 1 & 0 \\ -x_E & -y_E & -z_E & 1 \end{bmatrix} \qquad (4.3)$$

The new co-ordinate system is shown in Fig. 4.5.

(2) Rotating the co-ordinate system about the z-axis

Referring to Fig. 4.5 we now rotate the co-ordinate system about the z-axis through the angle $\frac{1}{2}\pi - \theta$ in the negative sense. This has the effect that the y-axis obtains the direction of the horizontal component of OE and that the x-axis becomes

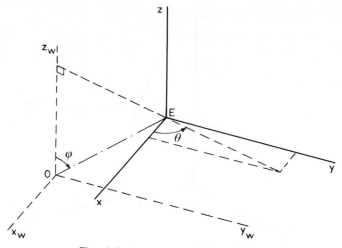

Fig. 4.5. New axes after translation

perpendicular to OE. The matrix for this change of co-ordinates is the same as for a rotation of points through the same angle in the positive sense. The 3×3 matrix for this rotation is:

$$R_z = \begin{bmatrix} \cos\left(\tfrac{1}{2}\pi - \theta\right) & \sin\left(\tfrac{1}{2}\pi - \theta\right) & 0 \\ -\sin\left(\tfrac{1}{2}\pi - \theta\right) & \cos\left(\tfrac{1}{2}\pi - \theta\right) & 0 \\ 0 & 0 & 1 \end{bmatrix}$$

$$= \begin{bmatrix} \sin\theta & \cos\theta & 0 \\ -\cos\theta & \sin\theta & 0 \\ 0 & 0 & 1 \end{bmatrix} \tag{4.4}$$

The new position of the axes is shown in Fig. 4.6.

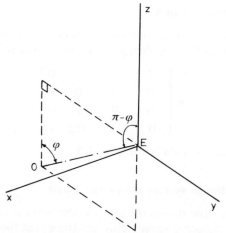

Fig. 4.6. New axes after rotation about z-axis

(3) Rotating the co-ordinate system about the x-axis

Since the z-axis is to have the direction EO we now rotate the co-ordinate system about the x-axis through the angle $\pi - \varphi$ in the positive direction. This corresponds to a rotation of points through the angle $-(\pi - \varphi) = \varphi - \pi$. Referring to Eq. (3.10) we have the following matrix:

$$R_x = \begin{bmatrix} 1 & 0 & 0 \\ 0 & \cos(\varphi - \pi) & \sin(\varphi - \pi) \\ 0 & -\sin(\varphi - \pi) & \cos(\varphi - \pi) \end{bmatrix}$$

$$= \begin{bmatrix} 1 & 0 & 0 \\ 0 & -\cos\varphi & -\sin\varphi \\ 0 & \sin\varphi & -\cos\varphi \end{bmatrix} \tag{4.5}$$

The new axes are shown in Fig. 4.7.

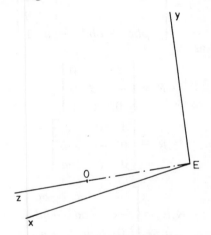

Fig. 4.7. New axes after rotation about x-axis

(4) Changing the direction of the x-axis

In Fig. 4.7 the y-axis and the z-axis have the right positions, but the x-axis is to point in the opposite direction. Thus we need the matrix for $x' = -x$, which is:

$$M_{yz} = \begin{bmatrix} -1 & 0 & 0 \\ 0 & 1 & 0 \\ 0 & 0 & 1 \end{bmatrix} \tag{4.6}$$

After this final transformation we have obtained the eye-co-ordinate system, already shown in Fig. 4.4.

We can now compute the viewing matrix V as the matrix product

$$V = TR_z^* R_x^* M_{yz}^* \tag{4.7}$$

where the notation R* is used for the 4×4 matrix obtained by extending a 3×3

matrix R with a fourth row and a fourth column containing the numbers 0, 0, 0, 1, in that order. Matrix multiplication is not commutative (in general, $AB \neq BA$), but it is associative, so we can write Eq. (4.7) as

$$V = T(R_z R_x M_{yz})^*$$

In this way we can deal with 3×3 matrices as long as possible. Our rather elaborate multiplication task is further relieved by introducing the abbreviations:

$$\begin{aligned} \cos \varphi &= a & \cos \theta &= c \\ \sin \varphi &= b & \sin \theta &= d \end{aligned} \tag{4.8}$$

Thus $a^2 + b^2 = 1$ and $c^2 + d^2 = 1$.

Using Eqs (4.1), we rewrite Eq. (4.3) as

$$T = \begin{bmatrix} 1 & 0 & 0 & 0 \\ 0 & 1 & 0 & 0 \\ 0 & 0 & 1 & 0 \\ -\rho bc & -\rho bd & -\rho a & 1 \end{bmatrix}$$

and Eqs (4.4) and (4.5) as

$$R_z = \begin{bmatrix} d & c & 0 \\ -c & d & 0 \\ 0 & 0 & 1 \end{bmatrix}$$

$$R_x = \begin{bmatrix} 1 & 0 & 0 \\ 0 & -a & -b \\ 0 & b & -a \end{bmatrix}$$

Hence

$$R_z R_x = \begin{bmatrix} d & -ac & -bc \\ -c & -ad & -bd \\ 0 & b & -a \end{bmatrix}$$

Post-multiplying this matrix by M_{yz} of Eq. (4.6) we obtain

$$R_z R_x M_{yz} = \begin{bmatrix} -d & -ac & -bc \\ c & -ad & -bd \\ 0 & b & -a \end{bmatrix}$$

We then find the desired viewing matrix V as the product of

$$T = \begin{bmatrix} 1 & 0 & 0 & 0 \\ 0 & 1 & 0 & 0 \\ 0 & 0 & 1 & 0 \\ -\rho bc & -\rho bd & -\rho a & 1 \end{bmatrix}$$

and

$$(R_z R_x M_{yz})^* = \begin{bmatrix} -d & -ac & -bc & 0 \\ c & -ad & -bd & 0 \\ 0 & b & -a & 0 \\ 0 & 0 & 0 & 1 \end{bmatrix}$$

Hence

$$V = \begin{bmatrix} -d & -ac & -bc & 0 \\ c & -ad & -bd & 0 \\ 0 & b & -a & 0 \\ v_{41} & v_{42} & v_{43} & 1 \end{bmatrix}$$

where

$$v_{41} = \rho bcd - \rho bcd = 0$$

$$\begin{aligned} v_{42} &= \rho abc^2 + \rho abd^2 - \rho ab \\ &= \rho\{ab(c^2 + d^2) - ab\} \\ &= \rho(ab - ab) \\ &= 0 \end{aligned}$$

$$\begin{aligned} v_{43} &= \rho b^2 c^2 + \rho b^2 d^2 + \rho a^2 \\ &= \rho\{b^2(c^2 + d^2) + a^2\} \\ &= \rho\{b^2 + a^2\} \\ &= \rho \end{aligned}$$

Thus we have found

$$V = \begin{bmatrix} -\sin\theta & -\cos\varphi\cos\theta & -\sin\varphi\cos\theta & 0 \\ \cos\theta & -\cos\varphi\sin\theta & -\sin\varphi\sin\theta & 0 \\ 0 & \sin\varphi & -\cos\varphi & 0 \\ 0 & 0 & \rho & 1 \end{bmatrix} \tag{4.9}$$

We have now derived an important result. If we are given the spherical co-ordinates ρ, θ, φ of viewpoint E we can compute the eye co-ordinates of a point from its world co-ordinates, using only Eqs (4.2) and (4.9).

The viewing transformation, which we have now dealt with, is to be followed by the perspective transformation in the next section. However, we could also use the eye co-ordinates x_e and y_e, simply ignoring z_e. In that case we have a so-called *orthographic projection*. Every point P of the object is then projected into a point P' by drawing a line from P, perpendicular to the plane through the x-axis and the y-axis. It can also be regarded as the perspective picture we obtain if the viewpoint is infinitely far away. An example of such a picture is the cube in Fig. 4.2(b). Parallel lines remain parallel in pictures obtained by orthographic projection. In practice such pictures are quite usual.

On the other hand, bringing some perspectivic effect into the picture will make it much more realistic. Our viewing transformation will therefore be followed by the perspective transformation, which will involve surprisingly little computation.

4.3 THE PERSPECTIVE TRANSFORMATION

The reader might have the impression that we are only half-way, and that this section will offer at least as much mathematics as Section 4.2. However, most of the work has been done. In this section the world co-ordinates will not be used. We shall therefore denote the eye co-ordinates by (x, y, z) instead of (x_e, y_e, z_e).

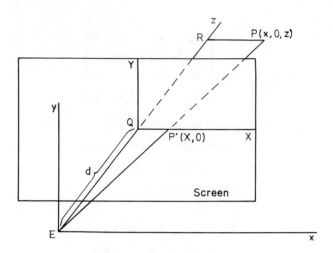

Fig. 4.8. Screen and eye co-ordinates

In Fig. 4.8 we have chosen a point Q, whose eye co-ordinates are $(0, 0, d)$ for some positive number d. The plane $z = d$ is the screen that we shall use. Thus the screen is the plane through Q and perpendicular to the z-axis. The screen-co-ordinate system is then determined by prescribing its origin to be Q and its X- and Y-axes to have the same directions as the x- and y-axes, respectively. For every object point P, the image point P' is the intersection of line PE and the screen. To keep Fig. 4.8 simple, we consider a point P whose y-co-ordinate is zero. However, the following equation to compute its screen co-ordinate X is also valid for other y-co-ordinates. In Fig. 4.8 the triangles EPR and EP'Q' are similar. Hence

$$\frac{P'Q}{EQ} = \frac{PR}{ER}$$

So we have

$$\frac{X}{d} = \frac{x}{z}$$

$$X = d \cdot \frac{x}{z} \tag{4.10}$$

In the same way we can derive

$$Y = d \cdot \frac{y}{z} \tag{4.11}$$

At the beginning of Section 4.2 we chose the origin O of the world-co-ordinate system to be a central point of the object. Since the z-axis of the eye-co-ordinate system is line EO, which intersects the screen in Q, the origin Q of the screen-co-ordinate system will be central in the image. If we require this origin to be in the bottom-left corner of the screen, and the dimensions of the screen are $2c_1$

horizontally and $2c_2$ vertically, we have to replace Eqs (4.10) and (4.11) with

$$X = d \cdot \frac{x}{z} + c_1 \qquad (4.12)$$

$$Y = d \cdot \frac{y}{z} + c_2 \qquad (4.13)$$

We still have to specify the distance d between viewpoint E and the screen. Roughly speaking, we have

$$\frac{picture\ size}{d} = \frac{object\ size}{\rho}$$

which follows from the similarity of the triangles EP'Q' and EPQ in Fig. 4.9. Thus we have

$$d = \rho \cdot \frac{picture\ size}{object\ size} \qquad (4.14)$$

This equation should be applied to both the horizontal and the vertical directions. It should be interpreted only as a means of obtaining an indication about an appropriate value for d, rather than as an exact prescription, since the three-dimensional object may have a complicated shape and it may not be clear how its size is to be measured. We then use a rough estimation of the object size, such as the maximum of its length, width and height. The picture size in Eq. (4.14) should be assumed to be somewhat smaller than the screen. More sophisticated methods to obtain a desired picture size will be discussed in Section 4.5.

The remaining part of this section is devoted to obtaining a better insight into concepts such as vanishing points and horizon. In Fig. 4.10 we have a viewpoint E and a screen ABCD. Again the viewing direction is from E to Q. Lines AF, BG, EH are parallel, and we consider them to be horizontal. We imagine a plane

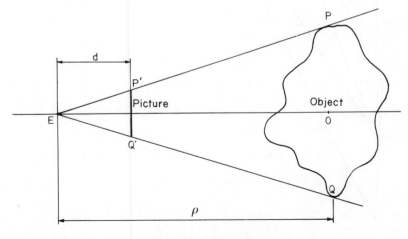

Fig. 4.9. Picture size

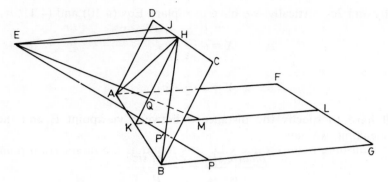

Fig. 4.10. Vanishing point H

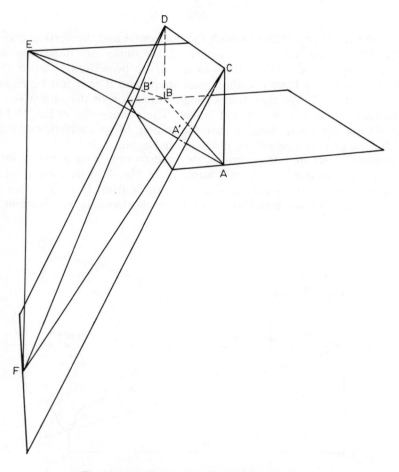

Fig. 4.11. Vanishing point F of vertical lines

through the parallel lines EH and BG. This plane and the screen have BH as a line of intersection. Thus every point P on BG has its central projection P' on BH, E being the centre of projection. If we let P move increasingly farther away from B, towards infinity, its projection P' will approach H. This means that H is the vanishing point of the line through B and G. In terms of projective geometry H is the projection of the infinite point of BG. As discussed in Section 3.6, parallel lines are said to meet in an infinite point. In Fig. 4.10 the parallel lines BG and AF have the same infinite point, so H is also the projection of the infinite point of AF. If we take a line with a different direction, but also horizontal, such as line BF, this line also has its vanishing point on line CD. It is found as the intersection point of line CD and a line through E parallel to the given horizontal line. Line CD is the horizon. Every point J of the horizon is the vanishing point of all lines that are parallel to EJ.

Not only horizontal lines have vanishing points. In Fig. 4.11 we have the vertical lines CA and DB. Point F is their vanishing point. It is the point where the vertical line through E meets the screen. Line segments CA and DB have projections CA' and DB', which are not parallel.

We do not always appreciate a strong perspective effect for vertical lines but we often prefer pictures where vertical lines are represented by almost vertical lines. This is so because we are accustomed to horizontal or nearly horizontal viewing directions. Some people even get dizzy if they look a long way vertically! Artists produce 'pseudo-perspective' pictures where vertical lines are represented by exactly vertical lines, even if the viewing direction is not horizontal. In the latter case, such a picture differs from what we actually see but, curiously enough, it seems to be all right. An example is Fig. 4.12(b). In Section 4.6 we shall revisit this phenomenon, and show that our programs are capable of producing such pseudo-perspective pictures (see Fig. 4.22(a)). In general, however, it is a good idea to choose a

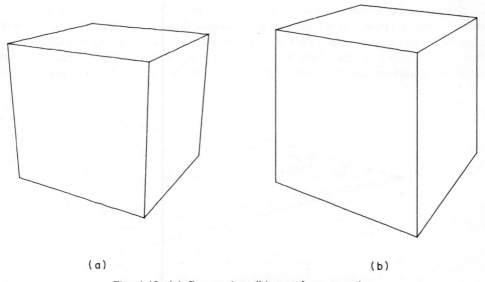

(a)   (b)

Fig. 4.12. (a) *Perspective*; (b) *pseudo-perspective*

Fig. 4.13. Ten cubes parallel to the screen

viewpoint not too close to the object, especially not if the angle φ indicated in Fig. 4.3 differs much from 90°. This is a practical way avoiding a strong perspective effect for vertical lines.

Another somewhat controversial subject is the representation of lines that are parallel to the screen. They will be represented by parallel lines in the picture. For example, consider Fig. 4.13, where we have ten cubes that are horizontally in line. The viewing direction is horizontal, so $\varphi = 90°$. This picture has a paradoxical aspect, which has to do with the size of the cubes. Cube A is more remote than cube E and yet these two cubes are the same size in the picture. This seems to be incorrect since remote objects ought to be represented as being smaller than near ones. Yet it is a central projection, obtained by rigorous geometric rules deserving our confidence. The paradox is solved by observing that Fig. 4.13 is unrealistic with respect to the way we view objects. The construction of our eye is such that we only see points within a certain cone, whose axis is the viewing direction EO. An important aspect of this cone is the angle α_{max} indicated in Fig. 4.14.

Eyes and cameras allow only α-values that do not exceed a certain α_{max}. Computationally, however, we have not limited the actual angle α, indicated in Fig. 4.14 and roughly satisfying

$$\tan \alpha = \frac{0.5 \cdot object\ size}{\rho}$$

so again a too-small choice of the viewing distance ρ is the source of the trouble. If we choose ρ large enough, the angle α will be sufficiently small to avoid the problems we discussed. If we are not yet satisfied there is another solution, namely to replace a flat screen with a part of a sphere whose centre is E. In this way we can allow large angles α, but then we no longer have flat pictures. These spherical pictures themselves can be projected into a plane. Readers who are interested in

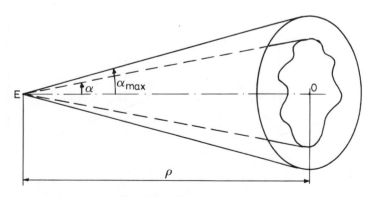

Fig. 4.14. Viewing cone

such unorthodox projection methods are referred to the work of the great graphical artist M. C. Escher (1972). We shall restrict ourselves to flat pictures and to rather small values of α.

4.4 A PROGRAM TO DRAW A CUBE

For many programming tasks we have to decide how general the program must be. There are two extreme possibilities. On the one hand, we can write a very special program, which does not read any input data and can only produce one result, say, some picture. On the other, we can develop a very general program, such as *GENPLOT* in Section 2.6, which can draw any picture provided that a file with input data be given. Between these extreme cases there are many possibilities for programs producing pictures of a certain type, after having read a limited amount of input data, sometimes called parameters.

In this section we shall develop a program to draw a perspective picture of a cube whose edges have length 100. This completely arbitrary size is no restriction whatsoever with respect to the picture, since the following parameters can freely be chosen.

(1) The three spherical co-ordinates (see Fig. 4.3):
   ρ, the viewing distance EO;
   θ, an angle, measured horizontally from the x-axis;
   φ, an angle, measured vertically from the z-axis.
(2) The distance d between the screen and the viewpoint.

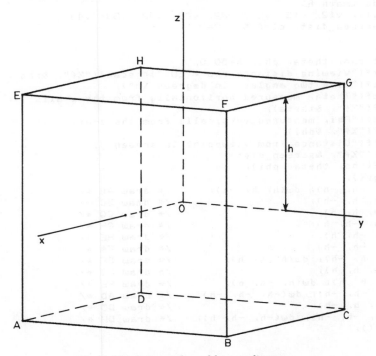

Fig. 4.15. Cube and world co-ordinates

The origin O of the world-co-ordinate system is chosen at the centre of the cube, as in Fig. 4.15. The length of each edge is denoted by $2h$, so $h = 50$. Then the vertices of the cube have the following co-ordinates:

$$A(\ h, -h, -h)$$
$$B(\ h, \quad h, -h)$$
$$C(-h, \quad h, -h)$$
$$D(-h, -h, -h)$$
$$E(\ h, -h, \quad h)$$
$$F(\ h, \quad h, \quad h)$$
$$G(-h, \quad h, \quad h)$$
$$H(-h, -h, \quad h)$$

We shall draw a so-called wire-frame model, which means that we do not distinguish visible and hidden lines. In our program it is as if we are moving a pen in three-dimensional space. We shall use the functions $mv(x, y, z)$ and $dw(x, y, z)$ in a similar manner as $move(x, y)$ and $draw(x, y)$ in two-dimensional space. In the functions mv and dw the function $perspective$ will be used, which performs both the viewing and the perspective transformation. For the sake of efficiency all coefficients not depending on the particular points A to H are computed beforehand by the function $coeff$. Here is the complete program:

```
/* CUBE: A wire frame model of a cube */
#include <math.h>
float v11, v12, v13, v21, v22, v23, v32, v33, v43,
      screen_dist, c1=4.5, c2=3.5;

main()
{ float rho, theta, phi, h=50.0;
  printf("Viewing distance rho = EO:"); scanf("%f", &rho);
  printf("Give two angles, in degrees.\n");
  printf("Theta, measured horizontally from the x-axis:");
  scanf("%f", &theta);
  printf("Phi, measured vertically from the z-axis:");
  scanf("%f", &phi);
  printf("Distance from viewpoint to screen:");
  scanf("%f", &screen_dist);
  coeff(rho, theta, phi);
  initgr();
  mv(h, -h, -h); dw(h, h, -h);        /* draw AB */
  dw(-h, h, -h);                      /* draw BC */
  dw(-h, h, h);                       /* draw CG */
  dw(-h, -h, h);                      /* draw GH */
  dw(h, -h, h);                       /* draw HE */
  dw(h, -h, -h);                      /* draw EA */
  mv(h, h, -h); dw(h, h, h);          /* draw BF */
  dw(-h, h, h);                       /* draw FG */
  mv(h, h, h); dw(h, -h, h);          /* draw FE */
  mv(h, -h, -h); dw(-h, -h, -h);      /* draw AD */
  dw(-h, h, -h);                      /* draw DC */
  mv(-h, -h, -h); dw(-h, -h, h);      /* draw DH */
  endgr();
}
```

```
coeff(rho, theta, phi) float rho, theta, phi;
{ float th, ph, costh, sinth, cosph, sinph, factor;
  factor=atan(1.0)/45.0;
  /* Angles in radians: */
  th=theta*factor; ph=phi*factor;
  costh=cos(th); sinth=sin(th);
  cosph=cos(ph); sinph=sin(ph);
  /* Elements of matrix V, see Eq. (4-9): */
  v11=-sinth; v12=-cosph*costh; v13=-sinph*costh;
  v21=costh;  v22=-cosph*sinth; v23=-sinph*sinth;
              v32=sinph;        v33=-cosph;
                                v43=rho;
}

mv(x, y, z) float x, y, z;
{ float X, Y;
  perspective(x, y, z, &X, &Y);
  move(X, Y);
}

dw(x, y, z) float x, y, z;
{ float X, Y;
  perspective(x, y, z, &X, &Y);
  draw(X, Y);
}

perspective(x, y, z, pX, pY) float x, y, z, *pX, *pY;
{ float xe, ye, ze;

  /* Eye coordinates, computed as in Eq. (4-2): */
  xe = v11*x + v21*y;
  ye = v12*x + v22*y + v32*z;
  ze = v13*x + v23*y + v33*z + v43;

  /* Screen coordinates, computed as    */
  /* in Eqs. (4-12) and (4-13):         */
  *pX = screen_dist*xe/ze + c1;
  *pY = screen_dist*ye/ze + c2;
}
```

This program actually produced the cubes in Fig. 4.16. Note that in the second picture we view the cube from the bottom and that in the third picture the projections of sides and diagonals happen to lie on the same lines. These cubes can only be recognized with some difficulty. Things would be much better if we had drawn solid objects instead of wire-frame models. This will be the topic of Chapter 5, where an algorithm is introduced to find out whether a line segment is visible

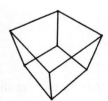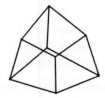

Fig. 4.16. Cubes seen from various viewpoints

from the viewpoint. However, if we take some care in choosing the viewpoint we can draw not too complicated solid objects by omitting hidden lines ourselves. For the cube in Fig. 4.15 this is done by choosing the viewpoint such that only the squares ABFE, BCGF, EFGH are visible and by omitting the edges AD, CD, DH. We then simply omit the three program lines immediately preceding *endgr*( ); in the program *CUBE*. The thus modified version of *CUBE* was actually used to produce Fig. 4.2(a), where $\rho = 200$, $\theta = 30$, $\varphi = 70$, $d = 3$, and Fig. 4.2(b), where $\rho = 200\,000$, $\theta = 30$, $\varphi = 70$, $d = 3000$.

4.5 DRAWING WIRE-FRAME MODELS

We shall now consider a program which can produce a perspective picture of any wire-frame model composed of finite straight line segments. By omitting certain line segments we can also produce pictures of simple solid objects, as we did for a cube in Section 4.4. As before, we shall use a viewpoint E and a 'object point' O, such that EO is the viewing direction. It would, however, not be convenient for the user to require this point O to be the origin of his world-co-ordinate system. We shall only require the user's z-axis to be vertical. The user will have to specify the co-ordinates x_O, y_O, z_O of object point O, expressed in his own co-ordinate system. When the user's co-ordinates are read, they are converted to 'internal world co-ordinates' x, y, z, with O as origin, according to:

$$x = \text{user's x-co-ordinate} - x_O$$
$$y = \text{user's y-co-ordinate} - y_O$$
$$z = \text{user's z-co-ordinate} - z_O$$

Then the user has to specify the spherical co-ordinates ρ, θ, φ, of viewpoint E, relative to the new origin O, as in Fig. 4.3. The distance d between viewpoint E and the screen must also be given. The position of the screen is then determined, since it is perpendicular to the viewing direction **EO**. To specify the line segments we again imagine movements in three-dimensional space that are associated with corresponding pen movements in the picture. For every move, a code

$$0 = pen\ up$$
$$1 = pen\ down$$

is given, which was also used in the file *A.SCRATCH* in Section 2.6. To draw the two adjacent line segments PQ and QR we have to specify three input lines of the following structure:

x_P	y_P	z_P	0	(move to P)
z_Q	y_Q	z_Q	1	(draw PQ)
x_R	y_R	z_R	1	(draw QR)

The right-hand side of each input line is comment, which actually may be present in the input file.

Before presenting the program we shall consider an example of a complete set of

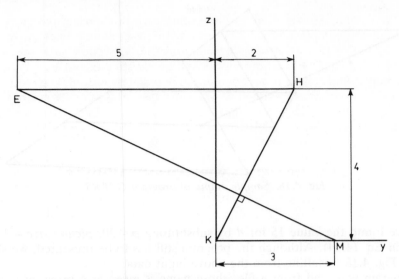

Fig. 4.17. View from positive x-axis

input data. Let us consider Fig. 4.10, which is not completely trivial. If we draw it by hand it is a problem to determine the position of point M on line KL, such that in three-dimensional space EM is perpendicular to plane BCDA. Let us take K as the origin of the user's co-ordinate system. We let the positive x-axis of this system pass through B and the positive y-axis through L. Viewed from the positive x-axis the yKz-plane is shown in Fig. 4.17. Three-dimensionally, K is in the middle of segment AB, whose length is 10. We can now give the complete set of input data for the picture we wish to draw:

0	2	2		(object point O)
30	−15	75	15	(rho, theta, phi, d)
5	0	0	0	(move to B)
5	2	4	1	(draw BC)
−5	2	4	1	(draw CD)
−5	0	0	1	(draw DA)
5	0	0	1	(draw AB)
5	9	0	1	(draw BG)
−5	9	0	1	(draw GF)
−5	0	0	1	(draw FA)
0	−5	4	0	(move to E)
0	2	4	1	(draw EH)
0	0	0	1	(draw HK)
0	9	0	1	(draw KL)
0	−5	4	0	(move to E)
0	3	0	1	(draw EM)

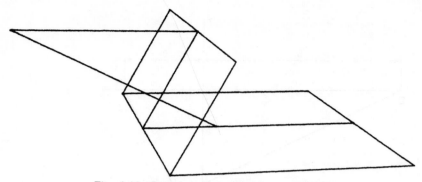

Fig. 4.18. Sample output of program GPERS

We have found the value 15 for *d* by substituting $\rho = 30$, *picture size* = 7, *object size* = 14 in Eq. (4.14). Although the program still has to be presented, we show its output in Fig. 4.18, resulting from the above input data.

The program will read from a file whose name is given as a program argument. This means that if the program name is *GPERS* and the file name is *PLANES*, we type

GPERS PLANES

instead of just *GPERS* in the command that starts the program execution. Programs with arguments usually have the line

*main(argc, argv) int argc; char *argv[ ];*

at the beginning of the function *main*. The program name, here *GPERS*, is also regarded as an argument. The argument count *argc* is the number of arguments (*argc* = 2 in the example) and the argument vector *argv* contains pointers to the arguments; in the example we have

argv[0] = "*GPERS*"

argv[1] = "*PLANES*"

The viewing and the perspective transformations are performed in the same way as in program *CUBE* in Section 4.4:

```
/* GPERS: General program for PERSpective */
#include <math.h>
#include <stdio.h>
float v11, v12, v13, v21, v22, v23, v32, v33, v43,
      screen_dist, c1=4.5, c2=3.5;

main(argc, argv) int argc; char *argv[];
{ float rho, theta, phi, x0, y0, z0, x, y, z;
  int code;
  FILE *fp;
  if (argc != 2) { printf("No file name given"); exit(1); }
  if (fp=fopen(argv[1],"r"), fp==NULL)
  { printf("File %s does not exist", argv[1]); exit(1);
  }
  fscanf(fp, "%f %f %f", &x0, &y0, &z0); skipf(fp);
  fscanf(fp, "%f %f %f %f", &rho, &theta, &phi, &screen_dist);
  coeff(rho, theta, phi);
  initgr();
  while (skipf(fp), fscanf(fp, "%f %f %f %d",
                            &x, &y, &z, &code) > 0)
    if (code) dw(x-x0, y-y0, z-z0); else mv(x-x0, y-y0, z-z0);
  endgr();
}


skipf(fp) FILE *fp; { while (getc(fp) != '\n'); }

coeff(rho, theta, phi) float rho, theta, phi;
{ float th, ph, costh, sinth, cosph, sinph, factor;
  factor=atan(1.0)/45.0;
  /* Angles in radians: */
  th=theta*factor; ph=phi*factor;
  costh=cos(th); sinth=sin(th);
  cosph=cos(ph); sinph=sin(ph);
  /* Elements of matrix V, see Eq. (4-9): */
  v11=-sinth; v12=-cosph*costh; v13=-sinph*costh;
  v21=costh;  v22=-cosph*sinth; v23=-sinph*sinth;
              v32=sinph;        v33=-cosph;
                                v43=rho;

}


mv(x, y, z) float x, y, z;
{ float X, Y;
  perspective(x, y, z, &X, &Y);
  move(X, Y);
}

dw(x, y, z) float x, y, z;
{ float X, Y;
  perspective(x, y, z, &X, &Y);
  draw(X, Y);
}
```

```
perspective(x, y, z, pX, pY) float x, y, z, *pX, *pY;
{ float xe, ye, ze;

    /* Eye coordinates, computed as in Eq. (4-2): */
    xe = v11*x + v21*y;
    ye = v12*x + v22*y + v32*z;
    ze = v13*x + v23*y + v33*z + v43;

    /* Screen coordinates, computed as     */
    /* in Eqs. (4-12) and (4-13):          */
    *pX = screen_dist*xe/ze + c1;
    *pY = screen_dist*ye/ze + c2;
}
```

The function *fscanf* delivers a non-positive value when a read attempt fails, that is, when the end of the file has been reached. Thus we want the loop to continue as long as *fscanf* returns a positive value.

The user of *GPERS* has to specify a value for the screen distance d. For the following reasons this is unsatisfactory:

(1) The user is interested in the picture size rather than in the screen distance.
(2) The 'object size' in Eq. (4.14) is a rather vague notion, so d cannot easily be determined in an exact way.
(3) We sometimes wish to specify a rectangular viewport, which might be only a part of our screen. Then the picture should fit into this viewport. It would be a nuisance if we had to convert viewport dimensions into a screen distance.

There are several ways of improving our program in this respect, namely:

(1) Clipping the three-dimensional object against the pyramid whose top is the viewpoint E and whose base is a certain window, given in world co-ordinates. For this method, which we shall not employ, the reader is referred to Newman and Sproull (1979).
(2) Clipping the picture two-dimensionally against a given viewport. We shall not use this method either.
(3) Adjusting the size and the position automatically, such that the picture fits exactly in a given viewport. We used this method for two-dimensional objects in Section 2.6, where the program *GENPLOT* acted as a post-processor, and we can use this program again. Moreover, we can consult the last thirteen lines of the program *CURVGEN* in Section 2.6, where plot data are written to the file *A.SCRATCH*.

We shall use method (3), using two files and two programs, as shown in Fig. 4.19.
Program *GPERSF* will not read the screen distance d but simply use the value

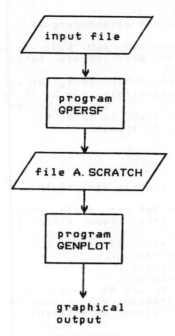

Fig. 4.19. Flowchart for GPERSF and GENPLOT

$d = 1$. This value is in fact irrelevant since the picture size computed by *GENPLOT* does not depend on d but on the given viewport. Recall that *GENPLOT* asks the user for the boundaries of the viewport. At this stage the reader might wonder if we can also get rid of the obligation to specify the object point O, since we have described O as a point central in the object and it seems that such a point can easily be computed automatically. However, there are two reasons to let O remain a point that the user has to specify. We shall discuss these reasons in Section 4.6.

The following program *GPERSF* accepts the same input file as *GPERS,* but the screen distance d at the end of the second line is ignored and may therefore be omitted.

```
/* GPERSF: General program for PERSpective, producing the   */
/*         output File A.SCRATCH, to be read by GENPLOT     */
#include <math.h>
#include <stdio.h>
float v11, v12, v13, v21, v22, v23, v32, v33, v43;

main(argc, argv) int argc; char *argv[];
{ float rho, theta, phi, x0, y0, z0, x, y, z;
  FILE *fpin, *fpout;
  struct { float X, Y; int code; } s;
  if (argc != 2) { printf("No input file given"); exit(1); }
  if (fpin=fopen(argv[1],"r"), fpin==NULL)
```

```
     { printf("File %s does not exist", argv[1]); exit(1);
     }
     fscanf(fpin, "%f %f %f", &x0, &y0, &z0); skipf(fpin);
     fscanf(fpin, "%f %f %f", &rho, &theta, &phi);
     coeff(rho, theta, phi);
     fpout=fopen("a.scratch", "w");   /* system dependent */
     while (skipf(fpin), fscanf(fpin, "%f %f %f %d",
                                     &x, &y, &z, &s.code) >0)
     { perspect(x-x0, y-y0, z-z0, &s.X, &s.Y);
       fwrite(&s, sizeof s, 1, fpout);
     }
     fclose(fpout);
}

skipf(fpin) FILE *fpin; { while (getc(fpin) != '\n'); }

coeff(rho, theta, phi) float rho, theta, phi;
{ float th, ph, costh, sinth, cosph, sinph, factor;
  factor=atan(1.0)/45.0;
  /* Angles in radians: */
  th=theta*factor; ph=phi*factor;
  costh=cos(th); sinth=sin(th);
  cosph=cos(ph); sinph=sin(ph);
  /* Elements of matrix V, see Eq. (4-9): */
  v11=-sinth;  v12=-cosph*costh;  v13=-sinph*costh;
  v21=costh;   v22=-cosph*sinth;  v23=-sinph*sinth;
               v32=sinph;         v33=-cosph;
                                  v43=rho;
}

perspect(x, y, z, pX, pY) float x, y, z, *pX, *pY;
{ float xe, ye, ze;

  /* Eye coordinates, computed as in Eq. (4-2):     */
  xe = v11*x + v21*y;
  ye = v12*x + v22*y + v32*z;
  ze = v13*x + v23*y + v33*z + v43;

  /* Screen coordinates, to be adjusted by GENPLOT */
  *pX = xe/ze;
  *pY = ye/ze;
}
```

The function *perspect* in this program has been derived from the function *perspective* of our previous programs *CUBE* and *GPERS*, by setting *screen_dist* = 1 and $c1 = c2 = 0$. (If other values had been chosen, the contents of file *A.SCRATCH* would have been different but the picture produced by *GENPLOT* would have been the same!)

4.6 VIEWING DIRECTION, INFINITY, VERTICAL LINES

We shall use the program *GPERSF* to discuss some interesting new aspects. Suppose that an object is very large in the x-direction, such as the beam in Fig. 4.20, whose dimensions are $200 \times 2 \times 2$. The interesting aspect of this example is the object point O that we must specify to determine the viewing direction EO. Up to now we have chosen O in the centre of the object. What we actually need, however, is a point O whose image point lies in the centre of the picture. Often this does not

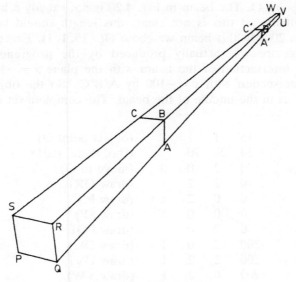

Fig. 4.20. Long beam

make much difference, but sometimes it does. The situation is illustrated in Fig. 4.21, where in the picture point O' lies in the middle of Q'U', but the original point O does not lie in the middle of QU. If the middle of QU had been chosen for O, the viewing direction would have differed significantly from the current viewing direction.

Returning to the beam in Fig. 4.20 it is clear that point O should not be chosen in the middle of the beam but much nearer to the eye. This is possible because in our programs the object point is given by the user rather than computed as the object centre. In the case of a landscape, finite line segments in the picture may result from infinite lines in reality. For such an infinite object it does not make sense to speak of an object centre, although there is a viewing direction EO, so it does make sense to

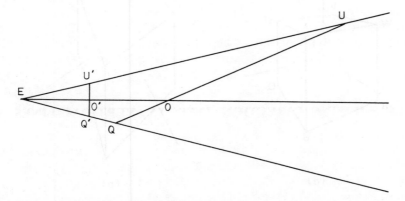

Fig. 4.21. Object point not in object centre

define an object point O. The beam in Fig. 4.20 is not exactly a landscape, but its length suggests infinity; if this is not clear, this length should be given a much greater value than 200. In this beam we chose $O(-15, 1, 1)$. Except for the letters $P, Q, \ldots$, this picture was actually produced by the programs *GPERSF* and *GENPLOT*. The intersection of the beam with the plane $x = -15$ is denoted by ABC, and the intersection with $x = -100$ by A'B'C'. So the object point lies in ABC, but A'B'C' is in the middle of the beam. The complete set of input data for Fig. 4.20 is:

−15	1	1		(object point O)
30	20	70		(rho, theta, phi)
0	2	0	0	(move to Q)
0	2	2	1	(draw QR)
0	0	2	1	(draw RS)
0	0	0	1	(draw SP)
0	2	0	1	(draw PQ)
−200	2	0	1	(draw QU)
−200	2	2	1	(draw UV)
−200	0	2	1	(draw VW)
0	0	2	1	(draw WS)
0	2	2	0	(move to R)
−200	2	2	1	(draw RV)
−15	2	0	0	(move to A)
−15	2	2	1	(draw AB)
−15	0	2	1	(draw BC)
−100	2	0	0	(move to A')
−100	2	2	1	(draw A'B')
−100	0	2	1	(draw B'C')

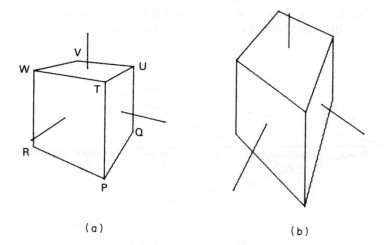

(a)   (b)

Fig. 4.22. (a) *Object point somewhat above the cube*; (b) *object point too far above the cube*

Another aspect deserving special attention is the representation of vertical lines, briefly discussed in Section 4.3. In Fig. 4.11 we saw the projected vertical lines meet in vanishing point F. We also compared the cube representations in Figs 4.12(a) and (b). If the object point O is placed in the centre of the cube our program cannot produce Fig. 4.12(b). However, we can place object point O above the cube such that the viewing direction EO is horizontal. The screen will then be vertical, since it is perpendicular to the viewing direction. This means that the vertical cube edges will be parallel to the screen. Their projections in the picture will therefore be exactly vertical. The curious aspect is that although the viewing direction is horizontal we view the upper plane of the cube from above. The picture that we obtain looks quite natural, unless we exaggerate and choose the viewpoint too high. Figures 4.22(a) and (b) show examples of both cases.

The lines in Fig. 4.22(a) were drawn by *GPERSF* and *GENPLOT,* using the following input data:

0	0	2		(point O)
5	30	90		(rho, theta, phi)
1	1	−1	0	(move to P)
−1	1	−1	1	(draw PQ)
−1	1	1	1	(draw QU)
1	1	1	1	(draw UT)
1	1	−1	1	(draw TP)
1	−1	−1	1	(draw PR)
1	−1	1	1	(draw RW)
1	1	1	1	(draw WT)
1	−1	1	0	(move to W)
−1	−1	1	1	(draw WV)
−1	1	1	1	(draw VU)
2	0	0	0	(x-axis)
1	0	0	1	
0	2	0	0	(y-axis)
0	1	0	1	
0	0	2	0	(z-axis)
0	0	1	1	

Figure 4.22(b) was obtained by choosing point O much higher, namely at $(0, 0, 6)$ instead of $(0, 0, 2)$. This is no longer a realistic picture of a cube. Figure 4.22(a), on the other hand, is quite acceptable. Some will even prefer it to the cubes in Figs 4.2(a) and 4.12(a), where vertical edges had a vanishing point. If a cube is perspectively drawn by hand it is customary to leave vertical lines vertical, as in Fig. 4.22(a). The other representations are more difficult to produce manually. With the computer they are produced just as easily and the user can choose what he likes.

REMARK

The programs in this chapter are meant to explain principles rather than to be used in practice. In Chapters 5 and 6 we shall discuss more practical programs.

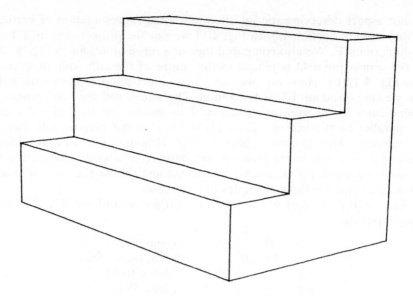

Fig. 4.23. Stairs

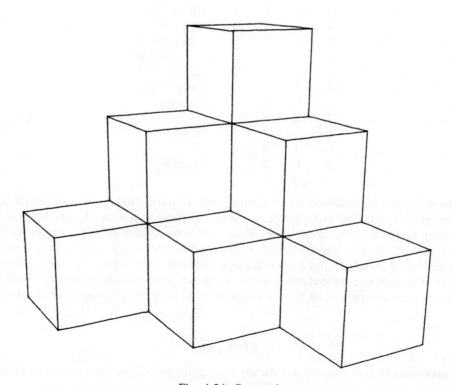

Fig. 4.24. Pyramid

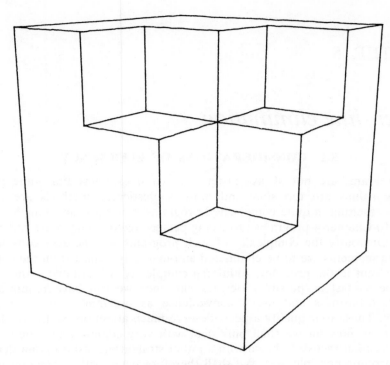

Fig. 4.25. Reduced cube

EXERCISES

In the following exercises hidden edges are to be omitted in the way we discussed at the end of Section 4.4.

4.1   Write a program to draw the stairs of Fig. 4.23. The number of stairs (n) should be variable ($n = 3$ in Fig. 4.23).

4.2   Write a program to draw a pyramid consisting of cubes, as in Fig. 4.24. The number n specifying the height of the pyramid in terms of cubes is to be read by the program ($n = 3$ in Fig. 4.24).

4.3   Write a program to draw the object of Fig. 4.25. This is a cube from which several small cubes have been removed. The dimensions of the small cubes are $1/n$ times those of the original one. The number n is variable ($n = 3$ in Fig. 4.25).

CHAPTER 5

Hidden-line elimination

5.1 CONSIDERATIONS OF EFFICIENCY

Simple programs are not always faster than complex ones. For some problems simple algorithms are too slow and more sophisticated methods are required, sometimes resulting in quite complicated programs. Sorting is an example of such a problem. In Chapter 4 programs producing perspective drawings were rather simple and fast. Obviously the complexity of such programs will increase considerably if hidden line segments are to be eliminated automatically. Apart from the complexity that is inherent in the problem, additional complexity is inevitable if the programs have to be as fast as possible. Besides efficiency we can have requirements of generality, robustness and user's convenience as potential sources of program complexity. These four quality aspects deserve much attention, so the reader might fear that from now on we shall only deal with very complicated programs. It is, however, more attractive to begin with a rather straightforward program than with a fast but incomprehensible one. We shall therefore begin with a program that is of n^2-time complexity. This means that computing time will be roughly proportional to n^2, where n is the number of line segments or the number of polygons that have to be drawn. The program will be fast enough to draw simple objects, but it cannot be used practically for objects having many hundreds of faces. We shall store the data describing the object in arrays of fixed sizes. This will also limit the object's complexity. Apart from these limitations, the program will be quite general: in principle, all finite objects that have only a finite number of flat faces can be drawn. As to robustness and user's convenience, we shall not require that all input errors, if any, should result in clear messages or that the object can be specified in the most convenient way. Later we shall improve the program, especially with respect to efficiency. Hidden-line elimination is a notoriously time-consuming task and a real challenge for programming mathematicians.

5.2 INPUT DATA AND INTERNAL REPRESENTATION

An edge of an object may be entirely or partly hidden by one or more of that object's faces. Every edge is a (finite) line segment. An object may consist of several parts, which need not be connected. In Fig. 5.1 we have a tetrahedron and a cube, whose vertices are assigned numbers 0, 1, 2, . . . instead of letters A, B, C, ... The assigned numbers 12, 13, 14 will enable us to draw the positive co-ordinate axes.

We intend to write a program that reads all data concerning the viewpoint and the object. For any (reasonable) viewpoint the graphical output will be the picture of the object. In contrast to Chapter 4, the object will be solid (and opaque). As in Section 4.5, the user has to supply two input lines specifying the rectangular

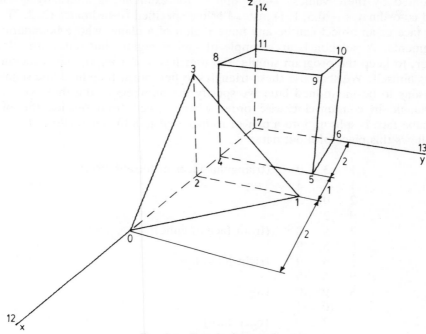

Fig. 5.1. Tetrahedron and cube

co-ordinates of the object point O and the spherical co-ordinates ρ, θ, φ of the viewpoint. In the example of Fig. 5.1 these input lines are

2.5	1	1	(object centre O)
8	20	70	(rho, theta, phi)

We did not intend to pay much attention to the user's convenience but we shall introduce the concept of coded vertices: we shall need each vertex several times and it would be extremely annoying if three co-ordinates had to be given each time. In this example we specify the vertex numbers 0 to 11, each followed by the x-, y- and z-co-ordinates of the vertex. A separate line with the character # in its first position denotes the end of this part of the input:

0	5	0	0	(x0 = 5, y0 = 0, z0 = 0)	8	2	0	2
1	3	2	0	(x1 = 3, y1 = 2, z1 = 0)	9	2	2	2
2	3	0	0	(etc.)	10	0	2	2
3	3	0	2		11	0	0	2
4	2	0	0		12	7	0	0
5	2	2	0		13	0	4	0
6	0	2	0		14	0	0	3
7	0	0	0		#			

As in Section 4.5, the object point O is the origin of the world-co-ordinate system that is used internally. (Note the distinction between the letter O and the digit 0.) Since point O has co-ordinates (2.5, 1, 1), the co-ordinates of the points 0 to 14 are decremented by these values. Thus point 9, for example, is internally given the reduced co-ordinates $(-0.5, 1, 1)$ instead of the specified co-ordinates $(2, 2, 2)$.

Each face of an object can be any finite region of a plane, whose boundaries are line segments. A polygon is an example of such a region, but holes are allowed. However, to keep the program simple, the user has to decompose each region into triangles himself. We shall use these triangles to find out if they hide line segments. For reasons to be mentioned later we specify the numbers of the three vertices of each triangle in counter-clockwise order when viewed from outside the object. Every cube face is split up into a pair of triangles. Again the character # (on a new line) follows this piece of input data:

1	3	0	(triangular faces of tetrahedron)
1	2	3	
2	0	3	
0	2	1	
4	5	8	(front face of cube)
8	5	9	
5	6	9	(right-hand face)
9	6	10	
8	9	10	(top face)
8	10	11	
6	7	10	(back face)
10	7	11	
7	4	8	(left-hand face)
7	8	11	
6	5	4	(bottom face)
6	4	7	
#			

Now every edge of the object has to be specified. Although these edges are already known as triangle sides they must be given again. First, not all triangle sides are object edges, and second, we appreciate the possibility of drawing additional line segments that do not belong to the solid object. To illustrate this we shall also draw parts of the positive co-ordinate axes, as in Fig. 5.1. Curiously enough, in the example this does not increase the number of input lines, since object edges that lie on the axes need not be specified again. Here are 17 input lines:

7	12	(x-axis)		5	6
7	13	(y-axis)		5	9
7	14	(z-axis)		8	9
0	1	(tetrahedron)		9	10
1	3			10	11
3	0			8	11
1	2			4	8
2	3			6	10
4	5	(cube)			

The program will read all input data from a file whose name is passed through the program arguments *argc* and *argv*, as in Section 4.5. The co-ordinates of each vertex are stored in the array *VERTEX*, whose elements are structures containing the three fields *x*, *y*, *z*. The given user's co-ordinates are first reduced to co-ordinates of a system whose origin is the object point O. These internal world co-ordinates are in turn converted to eye co-ordinates, by means of the viewing transformation discussed in Section 4.2. It is these eye co-ordinates that are stored in array *VERTEX*:

i	\multicolumn{3}{c}{*VERTEX[i]*}
↓	*x* ↓	*y* ↓	*z* ↓
0	.	.	.
1	.	.	.
.	.	.	.
.	.	.	.
.	.	.	.

As we know, E is the origin of the eye-co-ordinate system and the viewing direction is the positive z-axis. Therefore all values $VERTEX[i] \cdot z$ must be positive. We shall check this in the program and stop if the check fails.

A list of triangles is stored in the array *TRIANGLE*:

j	\multicolumn{7}{c}{*TRIANGLE[j]*}
↓	*A* ↓	*B* ↓	*C* ↓	*a* ↓	*b* ↓	*c* ↓	*h* ↓
0	.	.	.	.	.	.	.
1	.	.	.	.	.	.	.
.	.	.	.	.	.	.	.
.	.	.	.	.	.	.	.
.	.	.	.	.	.	.	.

Along with the vertex numbers of each triangle we store the coefficients *a*, *b*, *c*, *h* of the equation

$$ax + by + cz = h \tag{5.1}$$

of the plane in which the triangle lies. We could calculate them each time they are needed but that would mean a waste of time, since we shall need them quite often. (We write *h* rather than *d*, since we have used *d* for the distance between viewpoint E and the screen.) We choose *a*, *b* and *c* such that

$$a^2 + b^2 + c^2 = 1 \quad \text{and} \quad h \geqslant 0$$

Then we can write Eq. (5.1) as the inner product

$$\mathbf{n} \cdot \mathbf{x} = h$$

where

$$\mathbf{n} = [a \quad b \quad c]$$
$$\mathbf{x} = [x \quad y \quad z]$$

The so-called normal vector **n** is the vector of unit length that is perpendicular to the plane of the triangle. For any point X in that plane, vector $\mathbf{x} = \mathbf{EX}$ has the property that the inner product $h = \mathbf{n} \cdot \mathbf{x}$ is the distance between E and the plane.

Inner products were introduced in Section 3.2. Note that we are using the eye-co-ordinate system, with E as origin and EO as the positive z-axis. A plane parallel to the screen has the equation $z = h$, which is a special case of Eq. (5.1), with $a = b = 0$, $c = 1$. In the general case we compute a, b, c and h from the triangle vertices A, B, C. In Section 3.3 we saw that the plane through these points has the equation

$$\begin{vmatrix} x & y & z & 1 \\ x_A & y_A & z_A & 1 \\ x_B & y_B & z_B & 1 \\ x_C & y_C & z_C & 1 \end{vmatrix} = 0$$

We can write this equation as

$$\begin{vmatrix} y_A & z_A & 1 \\ y_B & z_B & 1 \\ y_C & z_C & 1 \end{vmatrix} x - \begin{vmatrix} x_A & z_A & 1 \\ x_B & z_B & 1 \\ x_C & z_C & 1 \end{vmatrix} y + \begin{vmatrix} x_A & y_A & 1 \\ x_B & y_B & 1 \\ x_C & y_C & 1 \end{vmatrix} z = \begin{vmatrix} x_A & y_A & z_A \\ x_B & y_B & z_B \\ x_C & y_C & z_C \end{vmatrix}$$

In the program, a, b, c and h are therefore computed as follows:

```
a = yA * (zB − zC) − yB * (zA − zC) + yC * (zA − zB);
b = −(xA * (zB − zC) − xB * (zA − zC) + xC * (zA − zB));
c = xA * (yB − yC) − xB * (yA − yC) + xC * (yA − yB);
h = xA * (yB * zC − yC * zB) −
    xB * (yA * zC − yC * zA) +
    xC * (yA * zB − yB * zA);
if (h > 0)
{ r = sqrt(a * a + b * b + c * c);
  a = a/r; b = b/r; c = c/r; h = h/r;
} else
{ ... /* We can ignore triangle ABC for the reasons */
      /* mentioned below.                           */
}
```

We save a considerable amount of time by computing a, b, c and h only once, instead of each time that a line segment is investigated on visibility.

If the program really had to be as simple as possible we would store all triangles that are read. However, triangles that are *backfaces* need not be stored but can be ignored. Consider triangle 123 in Fig. 5.1. In the picture this triangle is hidden by triangle 130. Since the latter triangle hides a part of line segment 45 we can ignore the fact that the former triangle does the same. A backface is hidden by visible faces. Although the backface can hide certain points from the eye, those visible faces also hide these points. This is why backfaces can be ignored. A simple way of determining whether a face is a backface is based on the orientation of the vertices. If we view the face 123 in Fig. 5.1 three-dimensionally from the outside (that is, from the negative x-axis) the order 123 in the input is counter-clockwise, since we have requested this orientation in the input sequence. In the picture of Fig. 5.1, however, the order 123 is clockwise. This means that in the picture this face is viewed through the body of the object instead of from the outside. Thus 123 is a backface. It is a good exercise to apply this decision method to other triangles in Fig. 5.1. Referring to the end of Section 3.4, we find that we require the determinant

$$D = \begin{vmatrix} X_A & Y_A & 1 \\ X_B & Y_B & 1 \\ X_C & Y_C & 1 \end{vmatrix}$$

where X_A, Y_A, X_B, Y_B, X_C, Y_C are the screen co-ordinates of the vertices A, B, C of the triangle. Triangle ABC is a backface if $D < 0$. We do not actually compute D, since we can write

$$D = \begin{vmatrix} x_A/z_A & y_A/z_A & 1 \\ x_B/z_B & y_B/z_B & 1 \\ x_C/z_C & y_C/z_C & 1 \end{vmatrix} = \begin{vmatrix} x_A & y_A & z_A \\ x_B & y_B & z_B \\ x_C & y_C & z_C \end{vmatrix} \Big/ (z_A z_B z_C)$$

$$= h/(z_A z_B z_C) \tag{5.2}$$

Since z_A, z_B, z_C are positive, D has the same sign as h, computed in the part of the program above. If $h = 0$, plane ABC passes through the origin E; but E is also our viewpoint, so in this case triangle ABC will hide no line segment and will therefore not be stored in array *TRIANGLE*. If $h < 0$, determinant D is negative and triangle ABC is a backface. So we store triangle ABC in the array only if $h > 0$, or, in other words, if $D > 0$.

With the aid of vector products we could also have concluded directly from $h < 0$ that triangle ABC is a backface without using screen co-ordinates. We leave this as an exercise for the mathematically oriented reader.

5.3 A HIDDEN-LINE ALGORITHM

We shall now develop an important algorithm whose task is to draw a given line segment PQ as far as it is visible. (We shall often briefly write 'PQ' to denote 'line segment PQ', to be distinguished from 'line PQ', which is the infinite line through the points P and Q.) For each triangle ABC of the list stored in array *TRIANGLE* we have to investigate whether it hides PQ (or a part of it).

As before, E is the viewpoint. We shall say that triangle ABC hides point R if line segment ER intersects triangle ABC in a point, interior to both the line segment and the triangle. The sides are not interior points of a triangle, and the endpoints are not internal points of a line segment. Thus R is not hidden by triangle ABC if R itself is an interior point of the triangle; neither are points on a side of the triangle hidden by the triangle. If triangle ABC does not hide point R we shall say that R is visible with respect to ABC. If at most a finite number of points of line segment PQ are visible with respect to ABC, we shall say that ABC hides PQ. For example, in Fig. 5.1 triangle 130 hides line segment 12, although this triangle does not hide point 1. If a triangle does not hide PQ we may not conclude that all points of PQ are visible with respect to the triangle, since the triangle may partly hide PQ. A triangle *partly* hides PQ if it hides infinitely many points of PQ and if at the same time infinitely many points of PQ are visible with respect to the triangle.

If some triangle hides PQ we need not take the remaining triangles of the list into consideration, but we can immediately conclude that PQ is hidden and must not be drawn.

We shall discuss the visibility of a line segment PQ with respect to a triangle ABC in a more algorithmic way. We are given the eye co-ordinates x_P, y_P, z_P, x_Q, etc. of the five points P, Q, A, B, C and the coefficients a, b, c, h of the equation $ax + by + cz = h$ that represents the plane through A, B, C. All information about triangle ABC is stored in the array element *TRIANGLE*[j]. A key factor in our considerations will be the infinite pyramid, whose top is viewpoint E and whose planes pass through the sides AB, BC, CA of the triangle. This pyramid will briefly be referred to as 'the pyramid'. In the same way the term 'triangle' refers to triangle ABC.

Everything in the pyramid behind the triangle is invisible; all points in front of the triangle or outside the pyramid are visible (with respect to the triangle). In Fig. 5.2 line segment PQ intersects the pyramid in two points I and J. Subsegment IJ is invisible, PI and JQ are visible. (For the sake of brevity, we abbreviate 'visible with respect to ABC' to 'visible'.)

The complexity of our task lies in the great number of cases that we have to deal with. In the situation of Fig. 5.2 we can compute the position of I as follows. A vector representation of line PQ is

$$\mathbf{EP} + \lambda\mathbf{r}$$

where $\mathbf{r} = [r_1 \quad r_2 \quad r_3] = \mathbf{PQ}$

so
$$r_1 = x_Q - x_P$$
$$r_2 = y_Q - y_P$$
$$r_3 = z_Q - z_P$$

Thus point (x, y, z) belongs to line PQ if

$$x = x_P + \lambda r_1$$
$$y = y_P + \lambda r_2 \qquad\qquad (5.2)$$
$$z = z_P + \lambda r_3$$

For λ-values between 0 and 1, the point lies between P and Q.

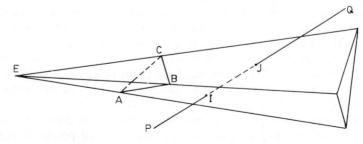

Fig. 5.2. The pyramid

The equation of plane EAB is

$$\begin{vmatrix} x & y & z \\ x_A & y_A & z_A \\ x_B & y_B & z_B \end{vmatrix} = 0$$

since it is an equation of a plane and it passes through the points $E(0, 0, 0)$, A, B. We write this equation as

$$C_1 x + C_2 y + C_3 z = 0 \tag{5.3}$$

where

$$C_1 = y_A z_B - y_B z_A$$
$$C_2 = x_B z_A - x_A z_B$$
$$C_3 = x_A y_B - x_B y_A$$

Substituting the right-hand sides of Eqs (5.2) into Eq. (5.3), we find:

$$\lambda = -\frac{(C_1 x_P + C_2 y_P + C_3 z_P)}{(C_1 r_1 + C_2 r_2 + C_3 r_3)} \tag{5.4}$$

Using this λ in Eq. (5.2) we obtain the co-ordinates of point I. The situation of Fig. 5.2 occurs only if λ lies between 0 and 1. For other values, point I does not lie on line segment PQ but on one of its extensions. We have not said that a value of λ between 0 and 1 implies that PQ intersects the pyramid, but only the reverse. Figure 5.3 shows a situation, viewed from E, where the value of λ lies between 0 and 1, although PQ does not intersect the pyramid.

Returning to the three-dimensional world of Fig. 5.2 we imagine a plane through line PQ and viewpoint E. We then want to know whether this plane passes through an interior point of AB. The calculations to find this out are similar to those that we used to find λ. A vector representation of line AB is

$$\mathbf{EA} + \mu \mathbf{AB}$$

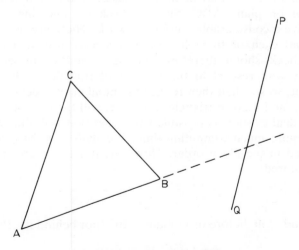

Fig. 5.3. PQ outside pyramid

Thus points (x, y, z) belongs to line AB if

$$
\begin{aligned}
x &= x_A + \mu(x_B - x_A) \\
y &= y_A + \mu(y_B - y_A) \\
z &= z_A + \mu(z_B - z_A)
\end{aligned}
\tag{5.5}
$$

For values of μ between 0 and 1, the point lies between A and B.

The equation of plane EPQ is

$$
\begin{vmatrix}
x & y & z \\
x_P & y_P & z_P \\
x_Q & y_Q & z_Q
\end{vmatrix} = 0
$$

We write this equation as

$$
K_1 x + K_2 y + K_3 z = 0
\tag{5.6}
$$

where

$$
\begin{aligned}
K_1 &= y_P z_Q - y_Q z_P \\
K_2 &= x_Q z_P - x_P z_Q \\
K_3 &= x_P y_Q - x_Q y_P
\end{aligned}
$$

Combining Eqs (5.5 and (5.6) we obtain

$$
\mu = -\frac{K_1 x_A + K_2 y_A + K_3 z_A}{K_1(x_B - x_A) + K_2(y_B - y_A) + K_3(z_B - z_A)}
\tag{5.7}
$$

Line segment PQ and pyramid plane EAB have a common point if and only if

$$
0 \leqslant \lambda \leqslant 1 \quad \text{and} \quad 0 \leqslant \mu \leqslant 1
$$

Up to now we have considered the intersection of PQ with only one pyramid plane, namely EAB. We also have to take the planes EBC and ECA into consideration. Line segment PQ may have zero, one or two intersections with the pyramid. The points P and Q may lie inside, outside or on the pyramid; they may lie before, behind or on plane ABC. Such a check for one line segment and one triangle will involve a considerable amount of work. There are usually a great many line segments, and each of them has to be checked against a great number of triangles. These checks should therefore be done efficiently. (In Section 5.4 we shall improve efficiency with respect to the number of triangles to be matched with a given line segment, so we shall then reduce the number of checks. Each check for a given line segment and a given triangle, however, will then be carried out as here.) It is attractive to deal as soon as possible with cases that will often occur, especially if they do not require much computing time. We shall now list a sequence of tests that are performed in the given order. However, if a test succeeds, the remaining tests should be ignored:

Test 1 (Fig. 5.4)

If both points P and Q lie before or in plane ABC (not behind it), PQ is visible. This happens if

$$
\mathbf{n} \cdot \mathbf{EP} \leqslant h \quad \text{and} \quad \mathbf{n} \cdot \mathbf{EQ} \leqslant h
$$

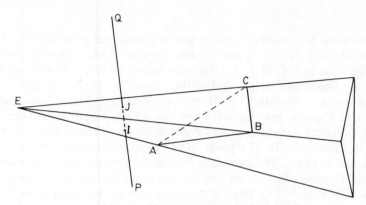

Fig. 5.4. Points P and Q not behind plane ABC

where $\mathbf{n} = [a \quad b \quad c]$. Recall that a, b, c, h occurred in Eq. (5.1) and are available in array element *TRIANGLE[j]*. Test 1 includes the important case that PQ is one of the sides of the triangle.

Test 2 (Fig. 5.5)

If (the infinite) line PQ lies outside the pyramid, PQ is visible. For this test we can substitute the co-ordinates of A, B and C in the left-hand side of Eq. (5.6), which denotes plane EPQ. If the three signs of the computed values (for A, B and C) are the same (all positive or all negative), points A, B, C lie on the same side of plane EPQ. Then line PQ lies outside the pyramid and is visible. We relax these sign conditions in the sense that one of the signs may be zero. We regard each sign as one of the numbers $-1, 0, 1$, and test whether the sum of the signs for A, B, C is one of the numbers $-3, -2, 2, 3$. Note that in Fig. 5.5(b) we could also have chosen point P coinciding with A. This, too, is an important special case.

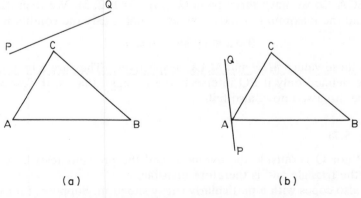

(a)   (b)

Fig. 5.5. (a) |sign sum| = 3; (b) |sign sum| = 2

Test 3

We now compute the intersections of line PQ with the planes EAB, EBC, EAC. We compute λ as in Eq. (5.4) for the intersection of line PQ with plane EAB; we also compute μ as in Eq. (5.7) for the intersection of line AB with plane EPQ. (In both cases the line might be parallel to the plane. We shall then assign a very large value to λ or μ.) Equation (5.3) denotes plane EAB. If we substitute the co-ordinates of P and C into the left-hand side of this equation and the results for P and C have different signs, the points P and C lie on different sides of AB. We then say that P lies beyond AB. If a point lies beyond one of the sides of the triangle it lies outside the triangle. We store this information in the logical variable *Poutside*. The variable *Qoutside* has an analogous meaning. We shall use these variables in Tests 4 and 6. If P and Q lie beyond the same side of the triangle, or if one of them lies beyond a side and the other precisely on that side, we say that PQ lies outside the triangle. Line segment PQ is then visible. Both situations are shown in Figs 5.6(a) and (b). An important special case arises if Fig. 5.6(b) is somewhat modified, such that point Q coincides with point A. Note that, unlike Fig. 5.5(b), the infinite line PQ in Fig. 5.6(b) may intersect BC between B and C. So Test 3 will succeed in cases where Test 2 has failed.

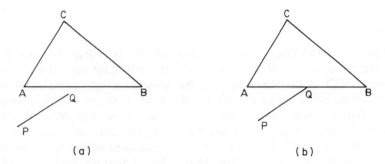

Fig. 5.6. (a) *Points P and Q beyond AB*; (b) *P beyond AB, Q on AB*

Most of the work has to be done three times, namely for each of the planes EAB, EBC and ECA, so we have three pairs (λ_l, μ_l) $(l = 1, 2, 3)$. We then determine the minimum and the maximum of those values λ_l that satisfy the condition

$$0 \leq \lambda \leq 1 \quad \text{and} \quad 0 \leq \mu \leq 1$$

and we call these values *MIN* and *MAX*, respectively. They are a by-product of this test and are defined only if PQ intersects the triangle, that is, if Test 3 fails and if Test 4, to be discussed now, also fails.

Test 4 (Fig. 5.7)

If neither P nor Q is outside the pyramid (and the previous tests have failed), PQ lies behind the triangle and is therefore invisible.

This test also copes with a particularly tricky situation. Suppose, for example, that PQ lies on the pyramid behind AB. Since PQ then lies neither outside nor inside the

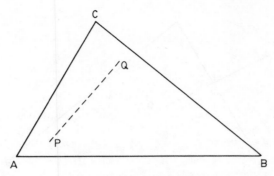

Fig. 5.7. PQ behind triangle ABC

pyramid, it seems doubtful whether we may say that the triangle hides PQ. However, AB may not be an edge but a diagonal of a face. Then that face does hide PQ, so PQ must not be drawn. On the other hand, should AB be an edge of the object, then PQ need not be drawn, since in the picture PQ would lie on AB and it does not make sense to draw coinciding line segments.

Test 5 (Fig. 5.8)

If a point I, where PQ intersects the pyramid, lies in front of the triangle, PQ is visible. This test is based on the fact that the object is solid, so PQ cannot pass through an interior point of the triangle. To find such points I we use the λ-values *MIN* and *MAX*, computed in Test 3. We can then simply test whether the inner product of the vectors **EI** and $\mathbf{n} = [a \quad b \quad c]$ is less than h.

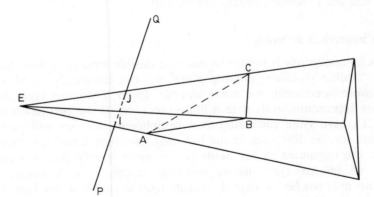

Fig. 5.8. Point of intersection in front of triangle ABC

Test 6

(This test is performed only if the previous tests have failed, that is, if PQ intersects the pyramid behind the triangle.)

If the λ-values *MIN* and *MAX* yield the points of intersection I and J, as in Fig.

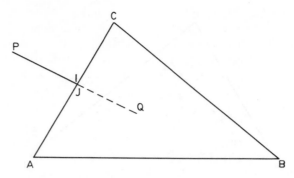

Fig. 5.9. Only one point of intersection

5.2, then IJ is invisible, and:

If P is outside the pyramid or before plane ABC, PI is visible.
If Q is outside the pyramid or before plane ABC, JQ is visible.

If P and Q do not both lie outside the pyramid, then points I and J will coincide. This is shown in Fig. 5.9.

In the previous tests if PQ was visible (with respect to the jth triangle), j was incremented by one. Line segment PQ was then checked against the remaining triangles, if there were any, or drawn if there were not. In this test, however, there may be two sub-segments PI and JQ that have to be checked against the remaining triangles. We can now recursively invoke our algorithm twice. For each recursive call, we specify the endpoints of the line segment and the number $j + 1$ of the triangle where the remaining checks are to start.

A note on numerical accuracy

In complex computations it is wise to use type *double* instead of *float*. Since *double* stands for 'double precision floating point' we can informally speak of 'floating point', if more specifically we mean *double*. Even if we use type *double*, real numbers are represented only with a finite precision. If the two numbers 5.843216 and 5.843217 have been calculated in a complicated way we will probably have consideration for the difference in the last digit, and regard both numbers as equal. If we wish the computer to act similarly, we must specify this in a precise way. Quantities of integer type are represented exactly. For floating-point types, however, this may not be the case. It is customary to choose a small positive value ε (for example, $\varepsilon = 10^{-6}$) and replace the test $x == a$ (for floating-point values x and a) with

$$fabs(x - a) <= epsilon, \qquad \text{or}$$
$$\cdot\, fabs(x - a) <= epsilon * fabs(a), \qquad \text{or}$$
$$fabs(x - a) <= epsilon + epsilon * fabs(a).$$

In the first test, *epsilon* is the absolute error that we admit. This test may cause problems for large values of a and x unless we use a somewhat larger *epsilon* in these cases. Since the magnitudes of x and a are usually unknown, we prefer a fixed value of *epsilon,* and consider replacing the first test with the second, where *epsilon* denotes the maximum relative error. However, if the value of a is (almost) zero the right-hand side of that inequality is (almost) zero, which is not exactly what we want. We shall therefore use the third test, where an absolute and relative error are combined. Obviously the third test reduces to the first if $a = 0$.

Summarizing, we perform tests on floating-point values x and a as shown in the following table, where we use $eps1 = epsilon + epsilon * fabs(a)$:

Instead of	We write
$x == a$	$fabs(x - a) <= eps1$
$x\ != a$	$fabs(x - a) > eps1$
$x < a$	$x < a - eps1$
$x <= a$	$x <= a + eps1$
$x > a$	$x > a + eps1$
$x >= a$	$x >= a - eps1$
$x == 0$	$fabs(x) <= epsilon$
$x\ != 0$	$fabs(x) > epsilon$
$x < 0$	$x < -epsilon$
$x <= 0$	$x <= epsilon$
$x > 0$	$x > epsilon$
$x >= 0$	$x >= -epsilon$

Note that the second half of this table can be derived from the first. In program *HIDLIN* below such tests will appear.

```
/* HIDLIN: A simple program for hidden-line elimination. */
/* The output of this program is the file A. SCRATCH,    */
/* which is to be read by GENPLOT.                       */
#include <stdio. h>
#include <math. h>
#define NVERTEX 200
#define NTRIANGLE 200
int ntr=0;
double v11, v12, v13, v21, v22, v23, v32, v33, v43,
  eps=1e-5, meps=-1e-5, oneminus=1-1. e-5, oneplus=1+1. e-5;
FILE *fpout;
struct { float X, Y; int code; } s;

struct { double x, y, z; } VERTEX [NVERTEX];
struct { int A, B, C; double a, b, c, h; }
                  TRIANGLE [NTRIANGLE];

main(argc, argv) int argc; char *argv[];
{ int i, j, A, B, C, P, Q;
   double x0, y0, z0, rho, theta, phi, x, y, z,
     xA, yA, zA, xB, yB, zB, xC, yC, zC,
     XA, YA, XB, YB, XC, YC, a, b, c, h, r;
```

```
     FILE *fpin;
     char ch;

     if (argc!=2 || (fpin=fopen(argv[1], "r"))==NULL)
       error("Input file not correctly specified");

     fscanf(fpin, "%lf %lf %lf", &x0, &y0, &z0); skipf(fpin);
     fscanf(fpin, "%lf %lf %lf", &rho, &theta, &phi);
     coeff(rho, theta, phi);
     while (skipf(fpin), ch=getc(fpin), ch!='#')
     { ungetc(ch, fpin);
       fscanf(fpin, "%d %lf %lf %lf", &i, &x, &y, &z);
       if (i<0 || i>=NVERTEX) error("illegal vertex number");
       viewing(x-x0, y-y0, z-z0,
           &VERTEX[i].x, &VERTEX[i].y, &VERTEX[i].z);
       if (VERTEX[i].z<=eps)
       { printf("Object point O and vertex %d lie on ", i);
         error("different sides of viewpoint E. ");
       }
     }

     while (skipf(fpin), ch=getc(fpin), ch!='#')
     { ungetc(ch, fpin);
       fscanf(fpin, "%d %d %d", &A, &B, &C);
       xA=VERTEX[A].x; yA=VERTEX[A].y; zA=VERTEX[A].z;
       xB=VERTEX[B].x; yB=VERTEX[B].y; zB=VERTEX[B].z;
       xC=VERTEX[C].x; yC=VERTEX[C].y; zC=VERTEX[C].z;
       a = yA * (zB-zC) - yB * (zA-zC) + yC * (zA-zB);
       b = -(xA * (zB-zC) - xB * (zA-zC) + xC * (zA-zB));
       c = xA * (yB-yC) - xB * (yA-yC) + xC * (yA-yB);
       h = xA * (yB*zC - yC*zB) -
           xB * (yA*zC - yC*zA) +
           xC * (yA*zB - yB*zA);
       if (h>0)
       { if (ntr == NTRIANGLE) error("Too many triangles");
         r = sqrt(a*a+b*b+c*c);
         a = a/r; b = b/r; c = c/r; h = h/r;
         TRIANGLE[ntr].A = A;
         TRIANGLE[ntr].B = B;
         TRIANGLE[ntr].C = C;
         TRIANGLE[ntr].a = a;
         TRIANGLE[ntr].b = b;
         TRIANGLE[ntr].c = c;
         TRIANGLE[ntr++].h = h;
       }
     /* If h=0, plane ABC passes through E and hides nothing. */
     /* If h<0, triangle ABC is a backface.                   */
     /* In both cases ntr is not incremented and the triangle */
     /* is not stored.                                        */
     }

     fpout=fopen("a.scratch", "w"); /* system dependent */
     if (fpout==NULL) error("file a.scratch cannot be opened");

     while (skipf(fpin), fscanf(fpin, "%d %d", &P, &Q) > 0)
       linesegment(VERTEX[P].x, VERTEX[P].y, VERTEX[P].z,
             VERTEX[Q].x, VERTEX[Q].y, VERTEX[Q].z, 0);
     fclose(fpout);
}

skipf(fpin) FILE *fpin; { while (getc(fpin) != '\n'); }
```

```
error(str) char *str; { printf("%s\n", str); exit(1); }

coeff(rho, theta, phi) double rho, theta, phi;
{ double th, ph, costh, sinth, cosph, sinph, factor;
  factor=atan(1.0)/45.0;
  /* Angles in radians: */
  th=theta*factor;  ph=phi*factor;
  costh=cos(th); sinth=sin(th);
  cosph=cos(ph); sinph=sin(ph);
  /* Elements of matrix V, see Eq. (4-9): */
  v11=-sinth;  v12=-cosph*costh;  v13=-sinph*costh;
  v21=costh;   v22=-cosph*sinth;  v23=-sinph*sinth;
               v32=sinph;         v33=-cosph;
                                  v43=rho;
}


viewing(x, y, z, pxe, pye, pze)
   double x, y, z, *pxe, *pye, *pze;
{ /* Eye coordinates, computed as in Eq. (4-2):      */
  *pxe = v11*x + v21*y;
  *pye = v12*x + v22*y + v32*z;
  *pze = v13*x + v23*y + v33*z + v43;
}


linesegment(xP, yP, zP, xQ, yQ, zQ, jO)
   double xP, yP, zP, xQ, yQ, zQ; int jO;
{ /* Line segment PQ is to be drawn, as far as it is   */
  /* not hidden by the triangles jO, jO+1, ..., ntr.   */
  int j=jO, worktodo=1, A, B, C, i, Pbeyond, Qbeyond,
     outside, Poutside, Qoutside, eA, eB, eC, sum;
  double a, b, c, h, hP, hQ, r1, r2, r3,
     xA, yA, zA, xB, yB, zB, xC, yC, zC,
     dA, dB, dC, MIN, MAX, lab, mu,
     xmin, ymin, zmin, xmax, ymax, zmax,
     C1, C2, C3, K1, K2, K3, denom1, denom2,
     Cpos, Ppos, Qpos, aux, eps1;
  while (j<ntr)
  { a=TRIANGLE[j].a; b=TRIANGLE[j].b; c=TRIANGLE[j].c;
    h=TRIANGLE[j].h; eps1=eps+eps*h;

/* Test 1: */
    hP=a*xP+b*yP+c*zP; hQ=a*xQ+b*yQ+c*zQ;
    if (hP<=h+eps1 && hQ<=h+eps1) {j++; continue;}
                                /* PQ not behind ABC */


/* Test 2: */
    K1=yP*zQ-yQ*zP; K2=zP*xQ-zQ*xP; K3=xP*yQ-xQ*yP;
    A=TRIANGLE[j].A; B=TRIANGLE[j].B; C=TRIANGLE[j].C;
    xA=VERTEX[A].x; yA=VERTEX[A].y; zA=VERTEX[A].z;
    xB=VERTEX[B].x; yB=VERTEX[B].y; zB=VERTEX[B].z;
    xC=VERTEX[C].x; yC=VERTEX[C].y; zC=VERTEX[C].z;
    dA=K1*xA+K2*yA+K3*zA;
    dB=K1*xB+K2*yB+K3*zB;
    dC=K1*xC+K2*yC+K3*zC;
   /* If dA, dB, dC have the same sign, the vertices A, B, C
      lie at the same side of plane EPQ.                  */
    eA= dA>eps ? 1 : dA<meps ? -1 : 0;
    eB= dB>eps ? 1 : dB<meps ? -1 : 0;
    eC= dC>eps ? 1 : dC<meps ? -1 : 0;
    sum = eA+eB+eC;
    if (abs(sum)>=2) { j++; continue; }
```

```
    /* If this test succeeds, the (infinite) line PQ
       lies outside pyramid EABC
       (at most one common point).
       If the test fails, there is a point
       of intersection.                                    */

/* Test 3: */
    Poutside=Qoutside=0; MIN=1.; MAX=0.;
    for (i=0; i<3; i++)
    { C1=yA*zB-yB*zA; C2=zA*xB-zB*xA; C3=xA*yB-xB*yA;
      /* C1 x + C2 y + C3 z = 0  is plane EAB */
      Cpos=C1*xC+C2*yC+C3*zC;
      Ppos=C1*xP+C2*yP+C3*zP;
      Qpos=C1*xQ+C2*yQ+C3*zQ;
      denom1=Qpos-Ppos;
      if (Cpos>eps)
      { Pbeyond= Ppos<meps; Qbeyond= Qpos<meps;
        outside= Pbeyond && Qpos<=eps ||
                 Qbeyond && Ppos<=eps;
      } else if (Cpos<meps)
      { Pbeyond= Ppos>eps; Qbeyond= Qpos>eps;
        outside= Pbeyond && Qpos>=meps ||
                 Qbeyond && Ppos>=meps;
      } else outside=1;
      if (outside) break;
      lab= fabs(denom1)<=eps  ? 1.e7 : -Ppos/denom1;
      /* lab indicates where PQ meets plane EAB */
      Poutside != Pbeyond;
      Qoutside != Qbeyond;
      denom2=dB-dA;
      mu= fabs(denom2)<=eps ? 1.e7 : -dA/denom2;
      /* mu tells where AB meets plane EPQ */
      if (mu>=meps && mu<=oneplus &&
          lab>=meps && lab<=oneplus)
      { if (lab<MIN) MIN=lab;
        if (lab>MAX) MAX=lab;
      }
      aux=xA; xA=xB; xB=xC; xC=aux;
      aux=yA; yA=yB; yB=yC; yC=aux;
      aux=zA; zA=zB; zB=zC; zC=aux;
      aux=dA; dA=dB; dB=dC; dC=aux;
    }
    if (outside) {j++; continue;}

/* Test 4: */
    if (!(Poutside || Qoutside))
    { worktodo=0; break; /* PQ invisible */
    }

/* Test 5: */
    r1=xQ-xP; r2=yQ-yP; r3=zQ-zP;
    xmin=xP+MIN*r1; ymin=yP+MIN*r2; zmin=zP+MIN*r3;
    if (a*xmin+b*ymin+c*zmin<h-eps1) { j++; continue; }
    xmax=xP+MAX*r1; ymax=yP+MAX*r2; zmax=zP+MAX*r3;
    if (a*xmax+b*ymax+c*zmax<h-eps1) { j++; continue; }

    /* If this test succeeds, an intersection of PQ
       and the pyramid lies in front of plane ABC.      */
```

```
/* Test 6: */
   if (Poutside || hP<h-eps1)
      linesegment(xP, yP, zP, xmin, ymin, zmin, j+1);
   if (Qoutside || hQ<h-eps1)
      linesegment(xQ, yQ, zQ, xmax, ymax, zmax, j+1);
   worktodo=0; break;
   }

   if (worktodo)
   { s.X=xP/zP; s.Y=yP/zP; s.code=0;
     fwrite(&s, sizeof s, 1, fpout);
     s.X=xQ/zQ; s.Y=yQ/zQ; s.code=1;
     fwrite(&s, sizeof s, 1, fpout);
   }
}
```

The input data of Section 5.2 was read by this program. The results written in the file *A.SCRATCH* were read by program *GENPLOT*, which produced Fig. 5.10.

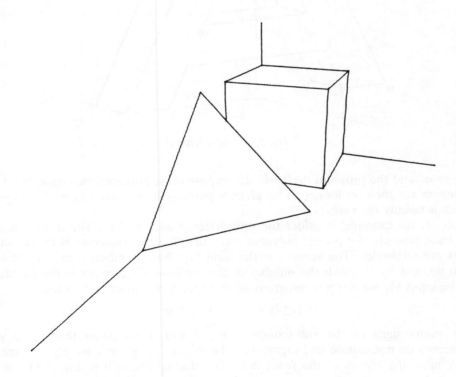

Fig. 5.10. Output of program HIDLIN

5.4 POLYGONS AND PIXELS

We shall now improve program *HIDLIN* of Section 5.3 with respect to the user's convenience and to efficiency. We shall enable the user to specify object faces as

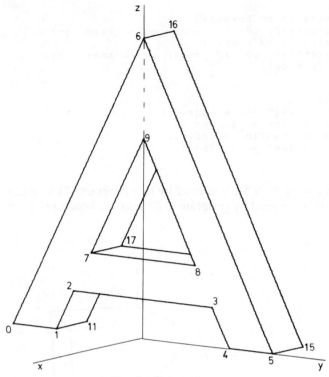

Fig. 5.11. Solid letter A

polygons[1] and the program itself will decompose these polygons into triangles. Line segments are then no longer to be given separately if they are edges of polygons, which is usually the case.

Let us, for example, consider the solid letter A of Fig. 5.11. The front face and the back face are not proper polygons since they have a triangular hole. All other faces are rectangles. The vertices in the front face have numbers 0 to 9. Increasing each number by 10 yields the number of the corresponding vertex in the backface. In the input file for our new program we can specify the front face as follows.

$$0\ 1\ 2\ 3\ 4\ 5\ 6\ -9\ 8\ 7\ 9\ -6$$

The minus signs in the sub-sequences 6 −9 and 9 −6 mean that these sub-sequences do not denote line segments to be drawn. They serve merely as a means of defining the region of the front face. The dashed line 6 9 in Fig. 5.11 can be regarded as two coinciding edges of a polygon. We obtain the front face in Fig. 5.11 if the distance d in the polygon of Fig. 5.12 becomes increasingly smaller. Instead of 6 9, other pairs of points could have been chosen to connect the outer and the inner boundaries. (However, we shall not write −0 since this does not represent a negative number.) The vertices must be listed in counter-clockwise order, with the exception of the inner boundary, where they are listed clockwise. The general rule is

[1] See the footnote in Section 3-5.

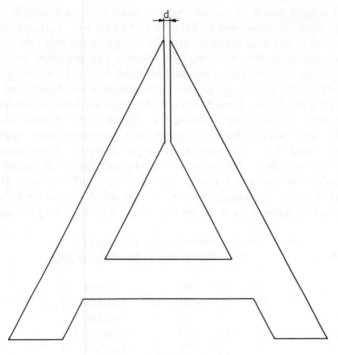

Fig. 5.12. A polygon

as follows. If we track the edges from vertex to vertex in the listed order, each time facing the next vertex, the region we are defining is to be on our left-hand side. This is why −9 in the above input sequence is followed by 8. If we move from vertex 9 to vertex 8 in Fig. 5.11, facing points 8, the 'material' of the letter A is on our left-hand side. Note that the input sequence is interpreted cyclically: the final vertex (6) is connected to the first vertex (0).

We shall require the first three vertices to enclose a convex angle. For example, we see in Fig. 5.11 that

$$1 \quad 2 \quad 3$$

at the beginning of the sequence would have been illegal, but

$$6 \quad 0 \quad 1$$

would have been acceptable.

The final vertex of every sequence must immediately be followed by the character #. This convention enables us to use several input lines for one sequence, so we can have polygons with a great many vertices. If a sequence contains only two vertices it is interpreted as a loose line segment. We use this facility, for example, to draw co-ordinate axes, as in Fig. 5.10.

As before, the file will begin with the co-ordinates

$$x \quad y \quad z$$

of the central object point O, which will be used as a new origin. The spherical co-ordinates ρ, θ, φ of viewpoint E, relative to O (see Fig. 4.3), will also be needed again, but instead of reading them from a file the program will now ask the user for these three numbers. In this way we can execute the program several times with different viewpoints without changing the file. Line EO is the viewing direction. The number of each vertex and its x-, y- and z-co-ordinates are again read from the file. Finally the vertex numbers of the faces are listed as we have discussed. Remember that we must view a face from outside the object to determine what is counter-clockwise. We shall adopt the convention that comment may appear anywhere outside numbers and that all comment be in parentheses. These parentheses must not be nested. To be able to determine where the last part of the input data begins it shall be preceded by the word Faces. (In fact we shall test only the first letter, capital F, and skip the remaining letters, so the word Facets could also be used.) The complete set of input data to draw the letter A of Fig. 5.11 is listed below.

<pre>
        0   0   30   (co-ordinates of point O;
                         the viewing direction is EO)
</pre>

<pre>
         0   0 -30   0   (vertex 0)
        10   -10 -30   0   (vertex 10)
         1   0 -20   0   (vertex 1)
        11   -10 -20   0   (vertex 11)
         2   0 -16   8   (vertex 2)
        12   -10 -16   8   (vertex 12)
         3   0   16   8   (vertex 3)
        13   -10   16   8   (vertex 13)
         4   0   20   0   (vertex 4)
        14   -10   20   0   (vertex 14)
         5   0   30   0   (vertex 5)
        15   -10   30   0   (vertex 15)
         6   0   0 60   (vertex 6)
        16   -10   0 60   (vertex 16)
         7   0 -12 16   (vertex 7)
        17   -10 -12 16   (vertex 17)
         8   0   12 16   (vertex 8)
        18   -10   12 16   (vertex 18)
         9   0   0 40   (vertex 9)
        19   -10   0 40   (vertex 19)
</pre>

Faces:

<pre>
         0   1   2   3   4   5   6   -9   8   7   9   -6#
        10   16 -19   17   18   19   -16   15   14   13   12   11#
         1   11   12   2#
         2   12   13   3#
        14   4   3   13#
         7   8   18   17#
</pre>

7	17	19	9#
18	8	9	19#
5	15	16	6#
10	0	6	16#
10	11	1	0#
14	15	5	4#

The program that we shall develop will be much more convenient than program *HIDLIN* in Section 5.3 since instead of triangles and line segments we can now directly specify object faces with complicated shapes. However, this is not the only improvement. In program *HIDLIN* we had a set of line segments and a set of triangles. Each line segment was matched with each triangle. Thus if the object increases in complexity in the sense that both sets become twice as large, computing time will increase by a factor 4. We say that *HIDLIN* has a quadratic time complexity.

For complex objects our new program will be much faster than *HIDLIN*. As before, we shall have a set of line segments and a set of triangles, but a given line segment will now be matched with only a sub-set of the set of triangles. For example, a line segment PQ that lies at the top left-hand part of the screen will not be matched with a triangle ABC in the bottom right-hand corner. To achieve this, we divide the screen into *Nscreen* × *Nscreen* rectangles of equal size, where *Nscreen* is some positive integer. In Fig. 5.13 we have chosen *Nscreen* = 8.

Such an elementary rectangle is called a *pixel*, which stands for picture element. Pixels are usually associated with raster-scan displays. To have an acceptable resolution, with such hardware many hundreds of pixels in both the horizontal and the vertical directions are required, since each pixel is then entirely filled with one

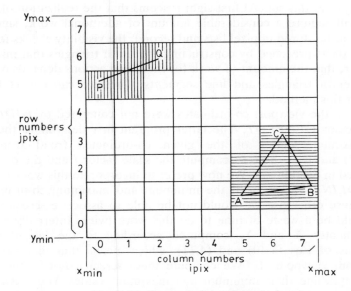

Fig. 5.13. Device-independent pixels

colour. Up to now, our approach has been device-independent. Perhaps contrary to what the reader will expect after the introduction of pixels, we shall stick to this principle! We are in fact using device-independent picture elements, so we could have invented a new name, such as *dipels*. Instead we shall conform to the usual terminology and use the term pixel. Note, however, that our pixels have nothing to do with resolution or with hardware. The choice of *Nscreen* (8 in Fig. 5.13) may influence computation time, but it will not influence the resulting picture. Good performance figures have been obtained by the value *Nscreen* = 30, which means that there are $30 \times 30 = 900$ pixels.

Our improvement of efficiency is based on the idea of setting up a list of triangles for each pixel. Such a pixel list will contain only those triangles that (partly or entirely) cover the pixel. Thus in Fig. 5.13 only the lists of the shaded pixels in screen columns 5, 6, 7 will contain triangle ABC. As in program *HIDLIN*, there will be one general array *TRIANGLE*, whose elements are structures containing the vertex numbers A, B, C and the coefficients *a, b, c, h* of the equation of plane ABC. Recall that the eye co-ordinates of vertex A are stored in array element *VERTEX[A]*, etc. Depending on the context, 'triangle ABC' means either the original triangle in three-dimensional space or its projection onto the screen. We shall say, for example, that triangle side AB in Fig. 5.13 lies in pixel columns 5, 6, 7; this will somewhat simplify our discussion, since otherwise we would have to talk about the central projection A′B′ of the original side AB. In the pixel lists we store only subscript values *j*, representing the triangle whose relevant characteristics can be found in *TRIANGLE[j]*. We shall say that the triangles that partly or entirely cover a pixel are *associated* with that pixel. When all pixel lists have been established we can start drawing line segments. For each line segment PQ we begin with building the set of all triangles associated with pixels that contain points of PQ. In Fig. 5.13 such pixels are shaded in columns 0, 1, 2. We shall then match PQ only with the triangles in this set. At first sight it seems that the realization of this rather simple idea will require a considerable amount of additional work, since first, all triangles have to be stored in pixel lists and second, the visibility checks for each line segment have to be preceded by constructing the set of triangles that might hide it. Note, however, that the amount of work for these two actions depends only linearly on the number of triangles and line segments. Thus we can expect linear time complexity for this method.

In Section 5.3 the viewport co-ordinates were not computed by *HIDLIN* but by the post-processor *GENPLOT*. The latter program first determines the minimum and the maximum values of the given co-ordinates (read from the file *A.SCRATCH*) and uses these to compute the scale factor *f* and the offsets *c*1 and *c*2, as discussed in Section 2.6. We now prefer to incorporate this work into our new program *HIDLINPIX*. We need the minimum and maximum co-ordinate values anyhow, because otherwise we would not be able to associate screen points with pixels. It would be a waste of time to do this work twice. Internally we shall use screen co-ordinates *X* and *Y*, computed according to the 'clean' perspective transformations of Eqs (4.10) and (4.11), which means that this screen is at a distance 1 from viewpoint E. We compute these screen co-ordinates as soon as possible to determine their minimum and maximum values *Xmin, Xmax, Ymin, Ymax*. This screen should not be confused with the viewport where the picture will eventually appear. The correspondence between screen and viewport follows from the viewport boundaries Xvp_min, Xvp_max, Yvp_min, Yvp_max, that the user is asked for when the program is executed. The following program fragment is closely related to Section 2.6 and shows what is actually computed:

$$Xrange = Xmax - Xmin;$$
$$Yrange = Ymax - Ymin;$$
$$Xvp\_range = Xvp\_max - Xvp\_min;$$
$$Yvp\_range = Yvp\_max - Yvp\_min;$$
$$fx = Xvp\_range/Xrange;$$
$$fy = Yvp\_range/Yrange;$$
$$f = (fx < fy \ ? \ fx : fy);$$
$$Xcentre = 0.5 * (Xmin + Xmax);$$
$$Ycentre = 0.5 * (Ymin + Ymax);$$
$$Xvp\_centre = 0.5 * (Xvp\_min + Xvp\_max);$$
$$Yvp\_centre = 0.5 * (Yvp\_min + Yvp\_max);$$
$$c1 = Xvp\_centre - f * X\_centre;$$
$$c2 = Yvp\_centre - f * Y\_centre;$$

The viewport co-ordinates Xvp and Yvp can then be computed from the screen co-ordinates X and Y as follows:

$$Xvp = f * X + c1;$$
$$Yvp = f * Y + c2;$$

It is interesting to compare this with Section 4.3, which reveals that scale factor f is nothing else but the distance d between the viewpoint E and the plane where we can imagine the viewport. Thus the screen and the viewport are two parallel planes (both perpendicular to the viewing direction EO), the former at a distance 1 and the latter at a distance $d = f$ from viewpoint E.

We shall use the viewport co-ordinates only in the actual 'plotting commands', that is, in the calls of the functions *move* and *draw*. Internally we use screen co-ordinates X and Y, lying between the computed boundaries $Xmin$, $Xmax$, $Ymin$, $Ymax$. It is this screen that is divided into $Nscreen \times Nscreen$ pixels. We shall now discuss the relationship between x and $ipix$, the column number of the pixel. The relationship between Y and the row number $jpix$ will be analogous. As Fig. 5.13 shows, we have

$$Xmin \leqslant X \leqslant Xmax$$
$$0 \leqslant ipix \leqslant Nscreen - 1$$

Theoretically, the horizontal dimension of a pixel is

$$deltaX = (Xmax - Xmin)/Nscreen$$

(We shall presently see that a slight correction to this equation is practical.) Then $ipix$ is obtained by truncating the value of

$$(X - Xmin)/deltaX$$

to an integer. This computation has the unpleasant consequence that the value

$X = Xmax$ will yield $ipix = Nscreen$, instead of the largest value $Nscreen - 1$ that is permitted. One solution would be to extend the screen with a column (and a row) which then would only be used for points on the line $X = Xmax$ (or $Y = Ymax$). For reasons of economy we shall not use this solution, but insist on having only $Nscreen$ pixel columns, ranging from 0 to $Nscreen - 1$. This can easily be accomplished by slightly increasing $deltaX$. We shall multiply it by $1 + epsilon$, where, as usual, epsilon has a small positive value, say 10^{-5}. Thus, as soon as $Xmin$, $Xmax$, $Ymin$, $Ymax$ are determined, we compute:

$$deltaX = (1 + epsilon) * Xrange / Nscreen;$$
$$deltaY = (1 + epsilon) * Yrange / Nscreen;$$

Then any time we want the pixel associated with point (X, Y) its position is obtained by:

$$ipix = (X - Xmin) / deltaX;$$
$$jpix = (Y - Ymin) / deltaY;$$

Note that truncation is performed implicitly in the C language whenever a floating-point value is assigned to an integer variable. Thus, declaring $ipix$ and $jpix$ of type int is all we have to do.

We shall also require the reverse operation:

$$X = Xmin + ipix * deltaX;$$

We thus find the X that corresponds to the left-hand boundary of pixel column $ipix$. The screen point (X, Y) in the centre of pixel $(ipix, jpix)$ is computed as follows:

$$X = Xmin + (ipix + 0.5) * deltaX;$$
$$Y = Ymin + (jpix + 0.5) * deltaY;$$

We shall now see how pixels can be used to store information about the triangles they are associated with. We use linear lists of nodes, and each node contains a triangle number jtr and a pointer to the next node, if there is one. If not, the pointer field will have the value $NULL$. The start pointer of each list is located in the two-dimensional array $SCREEN$. Pixel $(ipix, jpix)$ corresponds to $SCREEN[ipix][jpix]$.

For the sake of efficiency, some of the triangles associated with a pixel will be given special treatment. These special triangles are those that *completely* cover the pixel. (A triangle covers a pixel completely if the entire pixel lies within the triangle.) For a given pixel $(ipix, jpix)$ all these special triangles can be ignored except the one that is nearest to the viewpoint! Here the terms 'near' and 'distance of the triangle' refer to the point in three-dimensional space where the line through E and the centre of the pixel meets the triangle. If there are triangles that completely cover the pixel, the number identifying the nearest of them will also be stored in $SCREEN[ipix][jpix]$, along with the distance of this triangle. The fields for these two new items are called tr_cov and tr_dist. Figure 5.14 shows a typical set of triangles associated with a pixel.

During the process of storing triangles, the pixel can have the data structure shown in Fig. 5.15. Only triangles 18 and 23 cover the pixel completely. Since

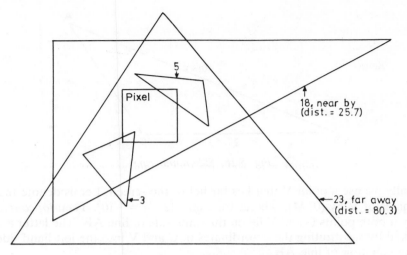

Fig. 5.14. Pixel and associated triangles

triangle 18 is the one that is nearer to the eye, its number and its distance are stored in the *SCREEN* element. Triangles 3 and 5 do not completely cover the pixel, therefore their distance does not matter at this stage. During the process of storing triangles, the nearest covering triangle, such as 18 in the example, is not immediately stored in the linear list since there might follow another triangle that covers the pixel and is nearer. At the end of this process the nearest covering triangle is added to the list. So finally the list of each pixel will contain all triangles that are associated with the pixel.

We now have to cope with an interesting programming problem. For a given triangle ABC, with screen co-ordinates *XA, YA, XB, YB, XC, YC,* we have to find out which pixels are associated with it and which of them, if any, are completely covered by it. This problem is far from trivial, because there are so many cases to consider. The first sub-problem is to determine for each of the three triangle sides whether it is a boundary at the top or at the bottom of the triangle. We assign the numbers 0, 1, 2 to the sides AB, AC, BC, respectively, as in Fig. 5.16. Here side 0 happens to be at the top and sides 1 and 2 at the bottom. Our intention is to code this as follows in array *topcode,* which has three elements:

$$topcode[0] = 1$$
$$topcode[1] = 0$$
$$topcode[2] = 0$$

So 1 and 0 are the codes for *top* and *bottom,* respectively. To determine these values

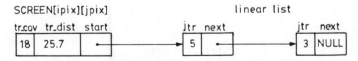

Fig. 5.15. Data structure for pixel

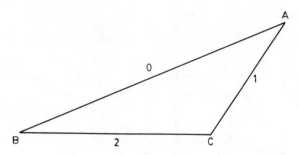

Fig. 5.16. Side numbering

analytically we use a point V that lies far below the screen. Let us denote the screen co-ordinates of V by $(0, M)$, where, for example, $M = -10^5$. Then $topcode[0] = 1$ if and only if both points C and V lie on the same side of line AB. The latter can easily be checked by substituting the co-ordinates of C and V into the left-hand side of the following equation of line AB:

$$\begin{vmatrix} x_A & y_A & 1 \\ x_B & y_B & 1 \\ x & y & 1 \end{vmatrix} = 0$$

If C and V yield the same sign in this substitution they lie on the same side of AB, which implies that AB is a top side. Thus in the C language we can briefly write

$$topcode[0] = (D * DAB > 0);$$

where D and DAB denote the determinants

$$D = \begin{vmatrix} x_A & y_A & 1 \\ x_B & y_B & 1 \\ x_C & y_C & 1 \end{vmatrix}$$

$$D_{AB} = \begin{vmatrix} x_A & y_A & 1 \\ x_B & y_B & 1 \\ 0 & M & 1 \end{vmatrix}$$

Analogous to this, we compute the determinants

$$D_{AC} = \begin{vmatrix} x_A & y_A & 1 \\ 0 & M & 1 \\ x_C & y_C & 1 \end{vmatrix}$$

$$D_{BC} = \begin{vmatrix} 0 & M & 1 \\ x_B & y_B & 1 \\ x_C & y_C & 1 \end{vmatrix}$$

and compute

$$topcode[1] = (D * DAC > 0);$$
$$topcode[2] = (D * DBC > 0);$$

Our next step is to determine the left-hand endpoint ($Xleft[l]$, $Yleft[l]$) and the right-hand endpoint ($Xright[l]$, $Yright[l]$) of each side l ($l = 0, 1, 2$). For example, in Fig. 5.16 we have $Xleft[0] = XB$, $Yleft[0] = YB$, etc.

We also determine the numbers *ipixmin* and *ipixmax* of the pixel columns where the extreme left and right vertices of triangle ABC lie. So for triangle ABC we have to update the pixel lists only for pixels in the columns $ipixmin, \ldots, ipixmax$. For each column *ipix* in this range we introduce the row boundaries $LOWER[ipix]$ and $UPPER[ipix]$. All pixels $LOWER[ipix], \ldots, UPPER[ipix]$ are associated with the triangle. A (possibly empty) sub-range of this is $LOW[ipix] + 1, \ldots, UP[ipix] - 1$. All pixels in this sub-range are completely covered by the triangle. Figure 5.17 shows the *l*th side of triangle ABC. Let us assume that this side is a bottom boundary, so $topcode[l] = 0$. Then this triangle side will contribute to the values of $LOWER[ipix]$ and $LOW[ipix]$ for the values of *ipix* in the range $ipixleft, \ldots, ipixright$, where the integers *ipixleft* and *ipixright* are truncated quotients, computed by:

$$ipixleft = (Xleft[l] - Xmin)/deltaX;$$
$$ipixright = (Xright[l] - Xmin)/deltaX;$$

We compute the slope of the triangle side:

$$slope = (Yright[l] - Yleft[l])/(Xright[l] - Xleft[l]);$$

(Contrary to the previous two assignments, no truncation will take place, since *slope* is a floating-point variable.) Proceeding from column *ipixleft* to column *ipixright* let us assume that we are dealing with column *ipix*. We are then interested in the row number *jI* of point I in Fig. 5.17, where the triangle side intersects the boundary between the pixel columns *ipix* and *ipix* + 1. This row number can be found through the screen co-ordinates (XI, YI) of intersection point I:

$$XI = Xmin + (ipix + 1) * deltaX;$$
$$YI = Yleft[l] + slope * (XI - Xleft[l]);$$
$$jI = (YI - Ymin)/deltaY; \quad /* \text{ implicitly truncated } */$$

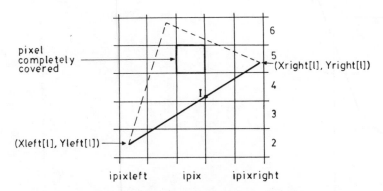

Fig. 5.17. Triangle side and pixel columns

Let j_old be the old value of jI, computed for column $ipix - 1$. Then we have

$$LOWER[ipix] = min(j\_old, jI);$$
$$LOW[ipix] = max(j\_old, jI);$$

where *min* is defined as the minimum value of its two arguments and *max* as their maximum value. In Fig. 5.17 we have $LOWER[ipix] = 3$, $LOW[ipix] = 4$. For pixel column *ipixleft*, we assign the truncated quotient $(Yleft[l] - Ymin)/deltaY$, being the row number of the left-hand endpoint, to j_old. Similarly, the truncated row number $(Yright[l] - Ymin)/deltaY$ of the right-hand endpoint is taken for jI in the column on the extreme right, *ipixright*. The above method is not yet correct in all cases. If in Fig. 5.18 the sides 0 and 1 are dealt with in that order we would obtain the wrong result $LOWER[ipix] = 6$, since the correct value 5, resulting from side 0, would be overwritten by the result from side 1. We shall therefore initially assign a very high value to the elements of array $LOWER$ and admit these elements only to be decremented. It can also be shown that the elements of LOW must be given very low initial values and only be incremented afterwards. The values of the arrays $UPPER$ and UP are determined analogously.

For triangle ABC (stored in $TRIANGLE[j]$) the column range $ipixmin, \ldots, ipixmax$ and the array elements $LOWER[ipix]$, $UPPER[ipix]$, $LOW[ipix]$, $UP[ipix]$ $(ipixmin \leq ipix \leq ipixmax)$ have now been determined, so we can now update matrix $SCREEN$ and the linear lists. If the range

$$LOW[ipix] + 1, \ldots, UP[ipix] - 1$$

is not empty, and *jpix* is a row number in this range, pixel $(ipix, jpix)$ is completely covered by triangle ABC. We are then interested in point R*, where the line through viewpoint E and centre R of the pixel intersects triangle ABC (see Fig. 5.19). Recall that plane ABC lies at a distance h from E and has $\mathbf{n} = [a \quad b \quad c]$ as its normal vector. The numbers a, b, c, h are available from $TRIANGLE[j]$. The component of **ER** in the direction **n** is **EQ**. The length EQ is therefore computed as

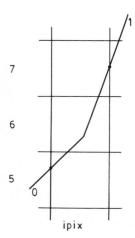

ipix   *Fig. 5.18. LOWER[ipix] depends on two triangles sides*

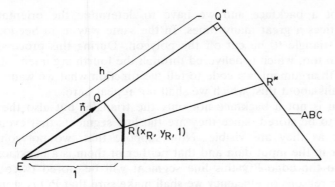

Fig. 5.19. Triangle distance

an inner product:

$$EQ = \mathbf{n} \cdot \mathbf{ER}$$
$$= [a \quad b \quad c] \cdot [x_R \quad y_R \quad 1]$$
$$= ax_R + by_R + c$$

Since the triangles ERQ and ER*Q* are similar, we have

$$\frac{ER^*}{EQ^*} = \frac{ER}{EQ}$$

Hence

$$ER^* = \frac{EQ^* \cdot ER}{EQ}$$

$$= \frac{h\sqrt{(x_R^2 + y_R^2 + 1)}}{ax_R + by_R + c}$$

The fields *tr_cov* of all matrix elements *SCREEN[ipix][jpix]* are initially set to -1, and all fields *tr_dist* are given the high initial value 10^{30}. For each pixel (*ipix, jpix*) that is completely covered by triangle *j* these two fields are updated if ER^* is less than the value already stored in *tr_dist*. The new triangle distance ER^* is then stored in field *tr_dist* and *j* is written in field *tr_cov*.

5.5 AN IMPROVED PROGRAM

In our program *HIDLINPIX* most of the new aspects are realized in function *counter_clock*. This is a quite complex function. Remember that the main differences between our previous program *HIDLIN* and this new program concern polygons and pixels. The decomposition of a polygon into triangles is carried out in essentially the same way as in Section 3.5. Every time a complete polygon has been read we test whether it is a backface. This test is applied to the triangle whose vertices are the first three vertices of the polygon. The test is similar to the one in program *HIDLIN* and is performed in function *counter_clock*, hence its name. If the first triangle turns out to be a backface, the entire polygon is ignored. Otherwise the polygon is not a backface and we have to determine the orientation of three successive vertices a great many times. In the same way as in Section 3.5 we thus find the next triangle to be cut off the polygon. During this process we want the diagonal length too, which is delivered through the fourth argument of the function. Finally, the fifth argument is a code to tell the function what we want. The program text gives details about this, which we shall not repeat here.

If a polygon is not a backface not only the triangles but also the edges of the polygon have to be stored, since they are the line segments that eventually will be drawn, as far as they are visible. Now suppose that two polygons PQRS and ABCQP occur in the input data and that neither of them is a backface. Since these polygons share the edge PQ this line segment will be stored twice if we do not prevent it. For reasons of efficiency we shall make sure that PQ is stored only once. This means that before storing PQ we have to search for it in the list of stored line segments; should it already be present in this list then we will not store it for the second time. All this has to be done efficiently with respect to time and space, since normally there are a considerable number of line segments. There are several ways to implement this. Instead of searching, it is attractive to use one of the vertex numbers of P and Q, say the less of them, as a subscript of an array. As in program *HIDLIN*, we have array *VERTEX*, where the rectangular co-ordinates of each vertex are stored. We now extend each element of this array with a pointer to an integer. Actually this pointer will point to the first of a sequence of integers. The C functions *malloc* and *realloc* enable us to allocate memory space only when we actually need it, in a very flexible way. The function *realloc* turns out to be especially useful here. Let us, for example, assume that, in this order, the following pairs of vertex numbers are given, each pair denoting a line segment to be stored if this has not to be done yet:

$$
\begin{array}{cc}
0 & 2 \\
1 & 3 \\
1 & 0 \\
0 & 1 \\
3 & 0
\end{array}
$$

This information will be stored as follows:

i	\multicolumn{4}{c}{$VERTEX[i]$}
↓	x	y	z	connect
0	. . .	. . .	. . .	$\longrightarrow$ 3 2 1 3
1	. . .	. . .	. . .	$\longrightarrow$ 1 3
2	. . .	. . .	. . .	$\longrightarrow$ 0
3	. . .	. . .	. . .	$\longrightarrow$ 0

The *connect* field of *VERTEX*[0], for example, points to the sequence 3, 2, 1, 3. The first 3 says that three vertex numbers will follow, namely for the line segments

$(0, 2)$, $(0, 1)$ and $(0, 3)$. In C notation we can write

$$ptr = VERTEX[0] \cdot connect; \qquad n = {}^*ptr;$$

In the example we have $n = 3$, and

$$*(ptr + 1) = 2 \qquad *(ptr + 2) = 1 \qquad *(ptr + 3) = 3$$

Note that when line segment 3 0 is to be stored this number sequence is converted to 0 3 for the sake of uniqueness. If it is not already present, it is then stored in the sequence starting in $VERTEX[0]$ instead of $VERTEX[3]$. The search for each line segment to be stored is now restricted to a usually small sequence, so this method will be fast. Since we allocate only memory that we actually need it is also economical with respect to space. In the program all this takes place in the function *add_linesegment*.

To a large extent program *HIDLINPIX* is similar to program *HIDLIN* of Section 5.3. This especially holds for the heart of the program, namely function *linesegment*. In *HIDLIN* this function had to match the given line segment PQ with all triangles. In *HIDLINPIX*, however, the set of triangles that have to be taken into consideration is usually much smaller. Before invoking function *linesegment* the main program builds this set on the basis of the given line segment PQ and the linear lists starting in matrix *SCREEN*. This is done in two steps. First, the arrays *LOWER* and *UPPER* are used again, but now to denote the pixels that line segment PQ passes through. This is done in a similar way as for triangles, so we shall not discuss this in detail. In the second step the pixels thus selected are used to find the triangles that they are associated with. If PQ passes through pixel ($ipix$, $jpix$), the triangles in the linear list starting in $SCREEN[ipix][jpix]$ are added to the set of triangles that we are building. The term 'set' is used here to emphasize that the array *trset* will contain each triangle number at most once. Suppose that $trset[0], \ldots, trset[ntrset - 1]$ is the sequence of triangles that we already have. (Initially $ntrset = 0$.) A new triangle number *trnr* is to be added to the sequence only if it does not yet occur in it. This is done by first placing it at the end:

$$trset[ntrset] = ntr;$$

as a so-called *sentinel*. We then search the sequence for *trnr*, starting at $trset[0]$. Since it will certainly be found, we need only test for equality to terminate the loop. After the loop is terminated, we test if $jnr = ntrset$. If so, we know that *jtr* did not yet occur in the sequence before we added it, and we increment *ntrset*. If $jtr < ntrset$, the triangle did already occur in the sequence, and *ntrset* is not incremented, which means that the sentinel is not effectively added to the set.

Here is the complete program *HIDLINPIX*:

```
/* HIDLINPIX: A program for hidden-line        */
/* elimination, using device-independent pixels.  */

#include <stdio.h>
#include <math.h>
#include <ctype.h>
```

```
#define max(x,y)     ((x)>(y)?(x):(y))
#define min(x,y)     ((x)<(y)?(x):(y))
#define max3(x,y,z)  ((x)>(y)?max(x,z):max(y,z))
#define min3(x,y,z)  ((x)<(y)?min(x,z):min(y,z))
#define xwhole(x)    ((int)(((x)-Xmin)/deltaX))
#define ywhole(y)    ((int)(((y)-Ymin)/deltaY))
#define xreal(i)     (Xmin+((i))*deltaX)


#define M -1000000.0
#define nvertex 1200
/* maximum number of vertices */
#define ntriangle 800
/* maximum number of (no backface) triangles to be stored */
#define Nscreen 30
#define big 1.e30;
#define NPOLY 400
/* maximum number of vertices of a single polygon */
#define nntrset 200
/* maximum size of set of triangles associated with
    a single (long) line segment                        */


int ntr=0, iaux, ipixmin, ipixmax, ipixleft, ipixright, ipix,
    jpix, jtop, jbot, j_old, l, jI, topcode[3], POLY[NPOLY],
    npoly,isize=sizeof(int), LOWER[Nscreen], UPPER[Nscreen],
    LOW[Nscreen], UP[Nscreen], trset[nntrset], ntrset;


double v11, v12, v13, v21, v22, v23, v32, v33, v43, d, c1, c2,
    eps=1e-5, meps=-1e-5, oneminus=1-1.e-5, oneplus=1+1.e-5,
    Xrange, Yrange, Xvp_range, Yvp_range, Xmin, Xmax, Ymin,
    Ymax, deltaX, deltaY, denom, slope,
    Xleft[3], Xright[3], Yleft[3], Yright[3];


char *malloc(), *realloc();

struct { double x, y, z; int *connect; } VERTEX [nvertex],
    *pvertex;

struct { int A, B, C; double a, b, c, h; }
                        TRIANGLE [ntriangle], *ptriangle;

struct node { int jtr; struct node *next; } *pnode;

struct { int tr_cov; double tr_dist; struct node *start; }
    SCREEN[Nscreen][Nscreen], *pointer;

    FILE *fpin;

/*-----------------------------------------------------------*/
main(argc, argv) int argc; char *argv[];
{ int i, P, Q, ii, imin, vertexnr,
    *ptr, iconnect, i0, i1, i2, code, count,
    trnr, jtr;

    double x0, y0, z0, rho, theta, phi, x, y, z,
        X, Y, xe, ye, ze,
        diag, min_diag, Xvp_min, Xvp_max, Yvp_min, Yvp_max,
        fx, fy, Xcentre, Ycentre, Xvp_centre, Yvp_centre,
        xP, yP, zP, xQ, yQ, zQ, XP, YP, XQ, YQ,
        Xlft, Xrght, Ylft, Yrght;
```

```
   char ch;

   if (argc!=2 || (fpin=fopen(argv[1], "r"))==NULL)
   { printf("Input file not correctly specified\n"); exit(1);
   }

/* Initialize screen matrix */
   for (ipix=0; ipix<Nscreen; ipix++)
   for (jpix=0; jpix<Nscreen; jpix++)
   { pointer=&(SCREEN[ipix][jpix]);
     pointer->tr_cov=-1; pointer->tr_dist=big;
     pointer->start=NULL;
   }

   reflo(&x0); reflo(&y0); reflo(&z0);
   printf("Give spherical coordinates rho, theta, phi of\n");
   printf("viewpoint E (phi = angle between z-axis and OE)\n");
   scanf("%lf %lf %lf", &rho, &theta, &phi);
   coeff(rho, theta, phi);
   init_viewport(&Xvp_min, &Xvp_max, &Yvp_min, &Yvp_max);

/* Initialize vertex array */
   for (i=0; i<nvertex; i++) VERTEX[i].connect=NULL;

/* Read vertices    */
   Xmin=Ymin=big; Xmax=Ymax=-big;
   while (skipbl(), ch=getc(fpin), ch!='F' && ch!='f')
   { ungetc(ch, fpin);
     reint(&i); reflo(&x); reflo(&y); reflo(&z);
     if (i<0 || i>=nvertex) error("Illegal vertex number");
     viewing(x-x0, y-y0, z-z0, &xe, &ye, &ze);
     if (ze <= eps)
     error(
"Object point O and a vertex on different sides of viewpoint");
     X=xe/ze;  Y=ye/ze;
     if (X<Xmin) Xmin=X; if (X>Xmax) Xmax=X;
     if (Y<Ymin) Ymin=Y; if (Y>Ymax) Ymax=Y;
     VERTEX[i].x=xe; VERTEX[i].y=ye; VERTEX[i].z=ze;
     VERTEX[i].connect = ptr = (int*)malloc(isize);
     if (ptr==NULL) error("Memory allocation error 1");
     *ptr=0;
   }


/* Compute screen constants */
   Xrange=Xmax-Xmin; Yrange=Ymax-Ymin;
   Xvp_range=Xvp_max-Xvp_min; Yvp_range=Yvp_max-Yvp_min;
   fx=Xvp_range/Xrange; fy=Yvp_range/Yrange;
   d=(fx<fy ? fx : fy);
   Xcentre=0.5*(Xmin+Xmax); Ycentre=0.5*(Ymin+Ymax);
   Xvp_centre=0.5*(Xvp_min+Xvp_max);
   Yvp_centre=0.5*(Yvp_min+Yvp_max);
   c1=Xvp_centre-d*Xcentre; c2=Yvp_centre-d*Ycentre;
   deltaX=oneplus*Xrange/Nscreen;
   deltaY=oneplus*Yrange/Nscreen;
   /* Now we have:  Xrange/deltaX < Nscreen */

/* Read object faces and store triangles */
   while (! isspace(getc(fpin)));
   /* The string "Faces: " has now been skipped */
```

```
  while (reint(&i)>0)
  { POLY[0]=i; npoly=1; skipbl();
    while (ch=getc(fpin), ch != '#')
    { ungetc(ch, fpin); reint(&POLY[npoly++]);
      if (npoly==NPOLY)
        error("Too many vertices in one polygon");
    }
    if (npoly==1) error("Only one vertex of polygon");
    if (npoly==2)
    { add_linesegment(POLY[0], POLY[1]);
      continue;
    }

    if (!counter_clock(0, 1, 2, &diag, 0)) continue;
                                         /* backface */

    for (i=1; i<=npoly; i++)
    { ii=i%npoly; code=POLY[ii]; vertexnr=abs(code);
      if (VERTEX[vertexnr].connect==NULL)
      error("Undefined vertex number used");
      if (code<0) POLY[ii]=vertexnr; else
        add_linesegment(POLY[i-1], vertexnr);
    }

    /* Division of a polygon into triangles,     */
    /* see Section 3-5:                          */

    count=1;
    while (npoly>2)
    { min_diag=big;
      for (i1=0; i1<npoly; i1++)
      { i0= (i1==0 ? npoly-1 : i1-1);
        i2= (i1==npoly-1 ? 0 : i1+1);
        if (counter_clock(i0, i1, i2, &diag,0) &&
                                      diag<min_diag)
        { min_diag=diag; imin=i1;
        }
      }
      i1=imin;
      i0= (i1==0 ? npoly-1 : i1-1);
      i2= (i1==npoly-1 ? 0 : i1+1);
/* store triangle in array TRIANGLE and in screen lists: */
      counter_clock(i0, i1, i2, &diag, count++);
      npoly--;
      for (ii=i1; ii<=npoly; ii++) POLY[ii]=POLY[ii+1];
    }
  }
  fclose(fpin);


/* Add nearest triangles to screen lists:  */
  for (ipix=0; ipix<Nscreen; ipix++)
  for (jpix=0; jpix<Nscreen; jpix++)
  { pointer=&(SCREEN[ipix][jpix]);
    if ((*pointer).tr_cov >= 0)
    { pnode=(struct node *)malloc(sizeof(struct node));
      if (pnode==NULL) error("Memory allocation error 2");
      pnode->jtr=pointer->tr_cov;
      pnode->next=pointer->start;
      pointer->start=pnode;
    }
  }
```

```
/* Draw all line segments as far as they are visible */
  for (P=0; P<nvertex; P++)
  { pvertex=VERTEX+P; /* = &VERTEX[P] */
    ptr = pvertex->connect;
    if (ptr == NULL) continue;
    xP = pvertex->x; yP = pvertex->y; zP = pvertex->z;
    XP= xP/zP; YP=yP/zP;
    for (iconnect=1; iconnect<=*ptr; iconnect++)
    { Q = *(ptr+iconnect);
      pvertex=VERTEX+Q; /* = &VERTEX[Q] */
      xQ = pvertex->x; yQ = pvertex->y; zQ = pvertex->z;
      XQ=xQ/zQ; YQ=yQ/zQ;

/* Using the screen lists, we shall build the    */
/* set of triangles that may hide points of PQ: */
      if (XP<XQ || (XP==XQ && YP<YQ))
      {Xlft=XP; Ylft=YP; Xrght=XQ; Yrght=YQ; } else
      {Xlft=XQ; Ylft=YQ; Xrght=XP; Yrght=YP; }
      ipixleft=xwhole(Xlft); ipixright=xwhole(Xrght);
      denom=Xrght-Xlft; if (fabs(denom)<=eps) denom=eps;
      slope=(Yrght-Ylft)/denom; jbot=jtop=ywhole(Ylft);
      for (ipix=ipixleft; ipix<=ipixright; ipix++)
      { if (ipix==ipixright) jI=ywhole(Yrght); else
                 jI=ywhole(Ylft+(xreal(ipix+1)-Xlft)*slope);
        LOWER[ipix]=min(jbot,jI); jbot=jI;
        UPPER[ipix]=max(jtop,jI); jtop=jI;
      }
      ntrset=0;
      for (ipix=ipixleft; ipix<=ipixright; ipix++)
      for (jpix=LOWER[ipix]; jpix<=UPPER[ipix]; jpix++)
      { pointer=&(SCREEN[ipix][jpix]);
        pnode= pointer->start;
        while (pnode!=NULL)
        { trnr= pnode->jtr;
/* trnr will be stored only if it is not yet */
/* present in array trset (the triangle set) */
          trset[ntrset]=trnr; /* sentinel */
          jtr=0;
          while (trset[jtr]!=trnr)jtr++;
          if (jtr==ntrset)
          { ntrset++; /* this means that trnr is stored */
            if (ntrset==nntrset)
                 error("Triangle set overflow");
          }
          pnode=pnode->next;
        }
      }
      /* Now trset[0], ..., trset[ntrset-1] is the set of */
      /* triangles that may hide points of PQ.            */

      linesegment(xP, yP, zP, xQ, yQ, zQ, 0);
    }
  }
  endgr();
}
```

```
/*------------------------------------------------------------*/
skipbl()
{ char ch;
  do ch=getc(fpin); while (isspace(ch)||comment(ch));
  ungetc(ch,fpin);
}
/*------------------------------------------------------------*/
int comment(ch) char ch;
{ int k;
  if (ch=='(')
  { do k=getc(fpin); while (k != ')' && k != EOF);
    return k==')';
  } else return 0;
}


/*------------------------------------------------------------*/
int reflo(px) double *px;
{ skipbl(); return fscanf(fpin, "%lf", px);
}

/*------------------------------------------------------------*/
int reint(pi) int *pi;
{ skipbl(); return fscanf(fpin, "%d", pi);
}

/*------------------------------------------------------------*/
add_linesegment(P, Q) int P, Q;
{ int iaux, *ptr, ii, n;
  if (P>Q) { iaux=P; P=Q; Q=iaux; }
  /* Now: P < Q */
  ptr=VERTEX[P].connect; n=*ptr;
  for (ii=1; ii<=n; ii++)
    if (*(ptr+ii)==Q) return; /* Q already in list */
  n++;
  VERTEX[P].connect=ptr=(int *)realloc(ptr, (n+1)*isize);
  if (ptr==NULL) error("Memory allocation error 3");
  *(ptr+n)=Q; *ptr=n;
}



/*------------------------------------------------------------*/
int counter_clock(i0, i1, i2, pdist, code)
    int i0, i1, i2, code; double *pdist;

/* code = 0: compute orientation; if counter-clockwise,     */
/*           compute length of projected diagonal AC        */
/* code = 1: compute a, b, c, h; store the first triangle    */
/* code > 1: check if next triangle is coplanar; store it    */

{ int A=abs(POLY[i0]), B=abs(POLY[i1]), C=abs(POLY[i2]);
  double xA, yA, zA, xB, yB, zB, xC, yC, zC, r,
         xdist, ydist, zdist,
         XA, YA, XB, YB, XC, YC, h0,
         DA, DB, DC, D, DAB, DAC, DBC, aux, dist,
         xR, yR;
  static double a, b, c, h;

  pvertex=VERTEX+A;
  xA = pvertex->x; yA = pvertex->y; zA = pvertex->z;

  pvertex=VERTEX+B;
  xB = pvertex->x; yB = pvertex->y; zB = pvertex->z;
```

```
pvertex=VERTEX+C;
xC = pvertex->x; yC = pvertex->y; zC = pvertex->z;
h0 = xA * (yB*zC - yC*zB) -
     xB * (yA*zC - yC*zA) +
     xC * (yA*zB - yB*zA);


if (code==0)
  if (h0>eps)
  { xdist=xC-xA; ydist=yC-yA; zdist=zC-zA;
    *pdist=xdist*xdist+ydist*ydist+zdist*zdist;
    return 1;
  } else return 0;
/* If h0=0, plane ABC passes through E and hides nothing.  */
/* If h0<0, triangle ABC is a backface.                    */
/* In both cases ntr is not incremented and the triangles  */
/* of the polygon are not stored.                          */


if (code==1)
{ a = yA * (zB-zC) - yB * (zA-zC) + yC * (zA-zB);
  b = -(xA * (zB-zC) - xB * (zA-zC) + xC * (zA-zB));
  c = xA * (yB-yC) - xB * (yA-yC) + xC * (yA-yB);
  r = sqrt(a*a+b*b+c*c); if (r==0.0) r=eps;
  a = a/r; b = b/r; c = c/r; h = h0/r;
} else if (fabs(a*xC+b*yC+c*zC-h)>0.001*fabs(h))
error(" Incorrectly specified polygon");
if (ntr == ntriangle) error("Too many triangles");
ptriangle=TRIANGLE+ntr; /* = &TRIANGLE[ntr] */
ptriangle->A = A; ptriangle->B = B ; ptriangle->C = C;
ptriangle->a = a; ptriangle->b = b ; ptriangle->c = c;
ptriangle->h = h;


/* The triangle will now be stored in the screen lists  */
/* of the associated pixels; first the arrays LOWER,    */
/* UPPER, LOW, UP are defined:                          */
XA=xA/zA; YA=yA/zA;
XB=xB/zB; YB=yB/zB;
XC=xC/zC; YC=yC/zC;
DA=XB*YC-XC*YB; DB=XC*YA-XA*YC; DC=XA*YB-XB*YA; D=DA+DB+DC;
DAB=DC-M*(XA-XB); DAC=DB-M*(XC-XA); DBC=DA-M*(XB-XC);
topcode[0]=(D*DAB>0); topcode[1]=(D*DAC>0);
topcode[2]=(D*DBC>0);
Xleft[0]=XA; Yleft[0]=YA; Xright[0]=XB; Yright[0]=YB;
Xleft[1]=XA; Yleft[1]=YA; Xright[1]=XC; Yright[1]=YC;
Xleft[2]=XB; Yleft[2]=YB; Xright[2]=XC; Yright[2]=YC;
for (l=0; l<3; l++) /* l = triangle-side number */
if (Xleft[l]>Xright[l] ||
   (Xleft[l]==Xright[l] && Yleft[l]>Yright[l]))
{ aux=Xleft[l]; Xleft[l]=Xright[l]; Xright[l]=aux;
  aux=Yleft[l]; Yleft[l]=Yright[l]; Yright[l]=aux;
}
ipixmin=xwhole(min3(XA,XB,XC));
ipixmax=xwhole(max3(XA,XB,XC));
for (ipix=ipixmin; ipix<=ipixmax; ipix++)
{ LOWER[ipix]=UP[ipix]=10000;
  UPPER[ipix]=LOW[ipix]=-10000;
}
```

```
  for (l=0; l<3; l++)
  { ipixleft=xwhole(Xleft[l]); ipixright=xwhole(Xright[l]);
    denom=Xright[l]-Xleft[l];
    if (ipixleft != ipixright) slope=(Yright[l]-Yleft[l])/denom;
    j_old=ywhole(Yleft[l]);
    for (ipix=ipixleft; ipix<=ipixright; ipix++)
    { if (ipix==ipixright) jI=ywhole(Yright[l]); else
         jI=ywhole(Yleft[l]+(xreal(ipix+1)-Xleft[l])*slope);
      if (topcode[l])
      { UPPER[ipix]=max3(j_old,jI,UPPER[ipix]);
        UP[ipix]=min3(j_old,jI,UP[ipix]);
      } else
      { LOWER[ipix]=min3(j_old,jI,LOWER[ipix]);
        LOW[ipix]=max3(j_old,jI,LOW[ipix]);
      }
      j_old=jI;
    }
  }


  /* For screen column ipix, the triangle is associated only */
  /* with pixels in the rows LOWER[ipix],...,UPPER[ipix].     */
  /* The subrange LOW[ipix]+1,...,UP[ipix]-1 of these rows    */
  /* denote pixels that lie completely whithin the triangle.  */

  for (ipix=ipixmin; ipix<=ipixmax; ipix++)
  for (jpix=LOWER[ipix]; jpix<=UPPER[ipix]; jpix++)
  { pointer=&(SCREEN[ipix][jpix]);
    if (jpix>LOW[ipix] && jpix<UP[ipix])
    { xR=Xmin+(ipix+0.5)*deltaX;
      yR=Ymin+(jpix+0.5)*deltaY;
      denom=a*xR+b*yR+c*d;
      dist= fabs(denom)>eps ? h*sqrt(xR*xR+yR*yR+1)/denom : big;
  /* The line from viewpoint E to pixel point (xR, yR, 1)  */
  /* intersects plane ABC at a distance dist from E.       */
      if (dist < pointer->tr_dist)
      { pointer->tr_cov=ntr; pointer->tr_dist=dist;
      }
    } else /* Add triangle to screen list: */
    { pnode=(struct node *)malloc(sizeof(struct node));
      if (pnode==NULL) error("Memory allocation error 4");
      pnode->jtr = ntr; pnode->next = pointer->start;
      pointer->start = pnode;
    }
  }
  ntr++;
}

/*----------------------------------------------------------*/
error(str) char *str; { endgr(); printf("%s\n", str); exit(1); }
```

```
/*------------------------------------------------------------*/
coeff(rho, theta, phi) double rho, theta, phi;
{ double th, ph, costh, sinth, cosph, sinph, factor;
  factor=atan(1.0)/45.0;
  /* Angles in radians: */
  th=theta*factor; ph=phi*factor;
  costh=cos(th); sinth=sin(th);
  cosph=cos(ph); sinph=sin(ph);
  /* Elements of matrix V, see Eq. (4-9): */
  v11=-sinth; v12=-cosph*costh; v13=-sinph*costh;
  v21=costh;  v22=-cosph*sinth; v23=-sinph*sinth;
              v32=sinph;        v33=-cosph;
                                v43=rho;
}


/*------------------------------------------------------------*/
viewing(x, y, z, pxe, pye, pze)
    double x, y, z, *pxe, *pye, *pze;
{ /* Eye coordinates, computed as in Eq. (4-2): */
  *pxe = v11*x + v21*y;
  *pye = v12*x + v22*y + v32*z;
  *pze = v13*x + v23*y + v33*z + v43;
}


/*------------------------------------------------------------*/
linesegment(xP, yP, zP, xQ, yQ, zQ, kO)
    double xP, yP, zP, xQ, yQ, zQ; int kO;
{ /* Line segment PQ is to be drawn, as far as it is not    */
  /* hidden by the triangles trset[kO] to trset[ntrset-1]. */
  int j, k=kO, worktodo=1, A, B, C, i, Pbeyond, Qbeyond,
    outside, Poutside, Qoutside, eA, eB, eC, sum;
  double a, b, c, h, hP, hQ, r1, r2, r3,
    xA, yA, zA, xB, yB, zB, xC, yC, zC,
    dA, dB, dC, labmin, labmax, lab, mu,
    xmin, ymin, zmin, xmax, ymax, zmax,
    C1, C2, C3, K1, K2, K3, denom1, denom2,
    Cpos, Ppos, Qpos, aux, eps1;
  while (k<ntrset)
  { j=trset[k];
    ptriangle=TRIANGLE+j; /* = &TRIANGLE[j] */
    a=ptriangle->a; b=ptriangle->b; c=ptriangle->c;
    h=ptriangle->h;

/* Test 1: */
    hP=a*xP+b*yP+c*zP; hQ=a*xQ+b*yQ+c*zQ;
    eps1=eps+eps*h;
    if (hP-h<=eps1 && hQ-h<=eps1) {k++; continue;}
                                /* PQ not behind ABC */
/* Test 2: */
    K1=yP*zQ-yQ*zP; K2=zP*xQ-zQ*xP; K3=xP*yQ-xQ*yP;
    A=ptriangle->A; B=ptriangle->B; C=ptriangle->C;
    pvertex=VERTEX+A;
    xA = pvertex->x; yA = pvertex->y; zA = pvertex->z;
    pvertex=VERTEX+B;
    xB = pvertex->x; yB = pvertex->y; zB = pvertex->z;
    pvertex=VERTEX+C;
    xC = pvertex->x; yC = pvertex->y; zC = pvertex->z;
    dA=K1*xA+K2*yA+K3*zA;
    dB=K1*xB+K2*yB+K3*zB;
    dC=K1*xC+K2*yC+K3*zC;
```

```
/* If dA, dB, dC have the same sign, the vertices        */
/* A, B, C lie at the same side of plane EPQ.            */
eA= dA>eps ? 1 : dA<meps ? -1 : 0;
eB= dB>eps ? 1 : dB<meps ? -1 : 0;
eC= dC>eps ? 1 : dC<meps ? -1 : 0;
sum = eA+eB+eC;
if (abs(sum)>=2) { k++; continue; }
/* If this test succeeds, the (infinite) line PQ         */
/* lies outside pyramid EABC (or the line and the        */
/* pyramid have at most one point in common.             */
/* If the test fails, there is a point                   */
/* of intersection.                                      */

/* Test 3: */
    Poutside=Qoutside=0; labmin=1.; labmax=0.;
    for (i=0; i<3; i++)
    { C1=yA*zB-yB*zA; C2=zA*xB-zB*xA; C3=xA*yB-xB*yA;
      /* C1 x + C2 y + C3 z = 0  is plane EAB */
      Cpos=C1*xC+C2*yC+C3*zC;
      Ppos=C1*xP+C2*yP+C3*zP;
      Qpos=C1*xQ+C2*yQ+C3*zQ;
      denom1=Qpos-Ppos;
      if (Cpos>eps)
      { Pbeyond= Ppos<meps; Qbeyond= Qpos<meps;
        outside= Pbeyond && Qpos<=eps ||
                 Qbeyond && Ppos<=eps;
      } else if (Cpos<meps)
      { Pbeyond= Ppos>eps; Qbeyond= Qpos>eps;
        outside= Pbeyond && Qpos>=meps ||
                 Qbeyond && Ppos>=meps;
      } else outside=1;
      if (outside) break;
      lab= fabs(denom1)<=eps  ? 1.e7 : -Ppos/denom1;
      /* lab indicates where PQ meets plane EAB */
      Poutside != Pbeyond;
      Qoutside != Qbeyond;
      denom2=dB-dA;
      mu= fabs(denom2)<=eps ? 1.e7 : -dA/denom2;
      /* mu tells where AB meets plane EPQ */
      if (mu>=meps && mu<=oneplus &&
          lab>=meps && lab<=oneplus)
      { if (lab<labmin) labmin=lab;
        if (lab>labmax) labmax=lab;
      }
      aux=xA; xA=xB; xB=xC; xC=aux;
      aux=yA; yA=yB; yB=yC; yC=aux;
      aux=zA; zA=zB; zB=zC; zC=aux;
      aux=dA; dA=dB; dB=dC; dC=aux;
    }
    if (outside) {k++; continue;}

/* Test 4: */
    if (!(Poutside || Qoutside))
    { worktodo=0; break; /* PQ invisible */
    }
```

```
/* Test 5: */
    r1=xQ-xP;  r2=yQ-yP;  r3=zQ-zP;
    xmin=xP+labmin*r1; ymin=yP+labmin*r2; zmin=zP+labmin*r3;
    if (a*xmin+b*ymin+c*zmin-h<-eps1) { k++; continue; }
    xmax=xP+labmax*r1; ymax=yP+labmax*r2; zmax=zP+labmax*r3;
    if (a*xmax+b*ymax+c*zmax-h<-eps1) { k++; continue; }

    /* If this test succeeds, an intersection of PQ
       and the pyramid lies in front of plane ABC.        */

/* Test 6: */
    if (Poutside !! hP<h-eps1)
      linesegment(xP, yP, zP, xmin, ymin, zmin, k+1);
    if (Qoutside !! hQ<h-eps1)
      linesegment(xQ, yQ, zQ, xmax, ymax, zmax, k+1);
    worktodo=0; break;
  }

  if (worktodo)
  { move(d*xP/zP+c1, d*yP/zP+c2);
    draw(d*xQ/zQ+c1, d*yQ/zQ+c2);
  }
}

/*------------------------------------------------------------*/
init_viewport(pXMIN,pXMAX,pYMIN,pYMAX)
  double *pXMIN, *pXMAX, *pYMIN, *pYMAX;
{ double XMIN, XMAX, YMIN, YMAX, len=0.2;
  printf("Give viewport boundaries XMIN, XMAX, YMIN, YMAX\n");
  scanf("%lf %lf %lf %lf", &XMIN, &XMAX, &YMIN, &YMAX);
  /* Show the four viewport corners:  */
  initgr();
  move(XMIN,YMIN+len);  draw(XMIN,YMIN);  draw(XMIN+len,YMIN);
  move(XMAX-len,YMIN);  draw(XMAX,YMIN);  draw(XMAX,YMIN+len);
  move(XMAX,YMAX-len);  draw(XMAX,YMAX);  draw(XMAX-len,YMAX);
  move(XMIN+len,YMAX);  draw(XMIN,YMAX);  draw(XMIN,YMAX-len);
  move((XMIN+XMAX)/2,YMIN);  draw((XMIN+XMAX)/2,YMIN);
  /* Dot in the middle of bottom viewport boundary
     for orientation.                                    */
  *pXMIN=XMIN; *pXMAX=XMAX; *pYMIN=YMIN; *pYMAX=YMAX;
}
```

If we apply this program to the input data at the beginning of Section 5.4, we obtain Fig. 5.20 as a result.

Fig. 5.20. Letter A in perspective

EXERCISES

5.1 Compose an input file for *HIDLINPIX* to draw a simple house in perspective.

5.2 Use *HIDLINPIX* for one of the Exercises of Chapter 4, but choose a fixed value for *n*, for example $n = 3$. In contrast to Chapter 4, we can now choose any viewpoint, without worrying about hidden edges.

5.3 Which modifications of *HIDLIN* (or *HIDLINPIX*) are needed if we wish to specify the viewpoint in *rectangular* co-ordinates?

5.4 In this chapter hidden line segments were completely omitted. However, engineers often represent them by dashed lines. Investigate how *HIDLIN* or *HIDLINPIX* can be modified to achieve this.

CHAPTER 6

Some applications

6.1 INTRODUCTION

Program *HIDLINPIX* is a general program to draw objects in perspective. However, despite the good facilities it offers compared with its *predecessor HIDLIN,* a considerable amount of work is still involved in preparing an input file. This task can be relieved in two ways. First, there are various types of devices for *graphic input* (see Newman and Sproull, 1979). We shall not discuss these but restrict ourselves to device-independent software. Second, we observe that many objects have a certain regularity, which enables us to produce the required file automatically. Programs for this purpose are executed before the main task, so they are sometimes called *pre-processors*. In this chapter we shall discuss some examples of such programs. They all generate a file, which is to be read by the program *HIDLINPIX*. As in Section 5.4, this file has the following structure:

$$xO \quad yO \quad zO \quad \text{(Co-ordinates of central object point)}$$
$$vertexnumber \quad x \quad y \quad z$$

$$vertexnumber \quad x \quad y \quad z$$
$$Faces: \qquad \qquad \text{(This keyword is required here)}$$
$$vertexnumber \quad \ldots \quad vertexnumber\# \qquad \text{(Polygon vertices)}$$

$$vertexnumber \quad \ldots \quad vertexnumber\#$$

Remarks

(1) Throughout the file we may insert comment between parentheses (. . .).
(2) After the keyword *Faces* the vertex numbers of each polygon are given in counter-clockwise order. The final vertex number of each polygon is *immediately* followed by the character #.
(3) If after *Faces* a sequence consists of only two vertex numbers, it denotes a simple line segment to be drawn (as far as it is visible). This facility enables us to draw line segments that are not object edges.
(4) If a face has a hole we transform it into a polygon by introducing an artificial edge. The latter will not be drawn if the second vertex number of the number pair for that edge is made negative. For example, if in Fig. 6.1 the inner

131

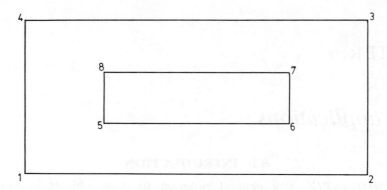

Fig. 6.1. Hole in rectangle

rectangle is a hole, we can introduce the artificial edge 2–6 and specify:

$$1 \ 2 \ -6 \ 5 \ 8 \ 7 \ 6 \ -2 \ 3 \ 4\#$$

Note that if we follow the edges in this order, facing the next vertex, we always find the region we are describing on our left-hand side. This means that the vertices of the hole are traversed clockwise instead of counter-clockwise.

In this introduction we shall draw a picture that is a logical extension of the example in Section 5.5. Instead of a single solid letter *A* we shall draw *n* copies of it in a row, where *n* can be any positive integer. In itself this picture is not likely to be of any value, but there is an aspect which we often encounter in practice, namely that a rather irregular portion of the picture (a single letter *A*) has a great many duplicates. Then the co-ordinates (and the vertex numbers) of the copies can be computed from the original. The following program is a pre-processor. It generates the file *A.DAT* to be read by *HIDLINPIX*. The program asks for the number of letters *A* to be drawn:

```
/* LETTERSA: A Preprocessor for HIDLINPIX  */
#include <stdio.h>
#define thickness 10
int base;
FILE *fp;
main()
{ int n, i, j, nr, x;
  static int X[20], /* By default initialized to 0 */
        Y[20] = {-30, -20, -16, 16, 20, 30,  0, -12, 12,  0},
        Z[20] = {  0,   0,  8,  8,  0,  0, 60,  16, 16, 40};
  printf("How many letters?\n");
  scanf("%d",&n);
  fp=fopen("a.dat", "w");
  fprintf(fp,"%f %f %f\n", -(n-0.5)*thickness, 0.0, 30.0);
  for (j=10; j<20; j++)
  { X[j] = -thickness; Y[j] = Y[j-10]; Z[j]= Z[j-10];
  }
  for (i=0; i<n; i++)
  for (j=0; j<20; j++)
  { nr = 20*i+j; x = -2*i*thickness+X[j];
    fprintf(fp, "%d %d %d %d\n", nr, x, Y[j], Z[j]);
  }
```

```
fprintf(fp, "Faces:\n");
for (i=0; i<n; i++)
{ base = 20*i;
  w12( 0,  1,  2,  3,  4,  5,  6, -9,  8,  7,  9, -6);
  w12(10, 16, -19, 17, 18, 19, -16, 15, 14, 13, 12, 11);
  w4( 1, 11, 12,  2);
  w4( 2, 12, 13,  3);
  w4(14,  4,  3, 13);
  w4( 7,  8, 18, 17);
  w4( 7, 17, 19,  9);
  w4(18,  8,  9, 19);
  w4( 5, 15, 16,  6);
  w4(10,  0,  6, 16);
  w4(10, 11,  1,  0);
  w4(14, 15,  5,  4);
}
fclose(fp);
}

w12(a, b, c, d, e, f, g, h, i, j, k, l)
  int a, b, c, d, e, f, g, h, i, j, k, l;
{ fprintf(fp,
    "%4d %4d %4d %4d %4d %4d %4d %4d %4d %4d %4d %4d#\n",
    s(a), s(b), s(c), s(d), s(e), s(f),
    s(g), s(h), s(i), s(j), s(k), s(l));
}

w4(a, b, c, d) int a, b, c, d;
{ fprintf(fp, "%4d %4d %4d %4d#\n", s(a), s(b), s(c), s(d));
}

int s(p) int p;
{ return p>=0 ? p+base : p-base;
}
```

To understand this program, see also Section 5.4, where the input file to draw a single letter A is given. In contrast to that file, lines of the type

vertexnumber   x   y   z

are now written in increasing order of vertex number, but this has no influence on the computation. To avoid repeated occurrences of somewhat tedious *fprintf* calls we have introduced the functions *w12* and *w4*. They in turn call the function *s*, which increments the local vertex numbers (<20) by $20i$, when dealing with the ith letter. Obviously this incrementation is replaced with a decrementation if the vertex number was made negative.

If this program is executed and we type 20 for the number of letters and 700, 80, 80 for the spherical co-ordinates of E, we obtain a quite extensive file $A.DAT$. Executing *HIDLINPIX* with this file gives the result shown in Fig. 6.2. The computing time on a PRIME 750 was about 17 s.

Fig. 6.2. Output produced by LETTERSA and HIDLINPIX

6.2   HOLLOW CYLINDER

Many objects are bounded by curved surfaces. We can often approximate such surfaces by polygons. An example is a hollow cylinder as shown in Fig. 6.3(b). For some sufficiently large integer n we choose n equidistant points on the outer circle (with radius R) of the top face and n similar points on the bottom face. Then we approximate the outer cylinder by a prism, whose vertices are these $2n$ points. There is also an inner cylinder, whose radius is r $(r < R)$. The two cylinders have height h and they share the z-axis of our co-ordinate system as their cylinder axes. The inner cylinder is approximated by a prism in the same way as the outer one. The bottom face lies in the plane $z = 0$ and the top face in the plane $z = h$. A vertex of the bottom face lies on the x-axis. For given values of n, R, r, h the object to be drawn and its position are then completely determined. We shall first deal with the case $n = 6$ and generalize this later for arbitrary n. We number the vertices as shown in Fig. 6.4.

For each vertex i of the top face $(1 \leq i \leq 12)$ there is a vertical edge that connects it with vertex $i + 12$. We can specify the top face by means of the following sequence:

$$1\ 2\ 3\ 4\ 5\ 6\ -12\ 11\ 10\ 9\ 8\ 7\ 12\ -6\#$$

Here the pairs $(6, -12)$ and $(12, -6)$ denote an artificial edge. In Fig. 6.4 the bottom face is viewed from the positive z-axis, but in reality only the other side is visible. For the bottom face the orientation is therefore the other way round, so that we specify:

$$18\ -24\ 19\ 20\ 21\ 22\ 23\ 24\ -18\ 17\ 16\ 15\ 14\ 13\#$$

Since $n = 6$, we have $12 = 2n$, $18 = 3n$ and $24 = 4n$, so the above sequences are special cases of:

$$1\ \ldots\ n\ -2n\ 2n - 1\ \ldots\ n + 1\ 2n\ -n\#$$

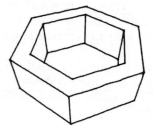

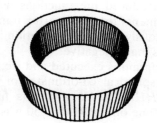

(a)   (b)

Fig. 6.3. (a) $n = 6$; (b) $n = 100$

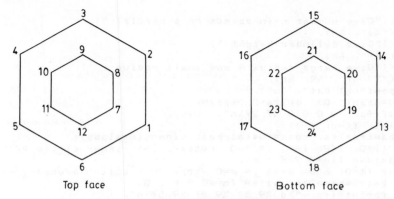

Fig. 6.4. Point numbering

and

$$3n \quad -4n \quad 3n+1 \; \ldots \; 4n \quad -3n \quad 3n-1 \; \ldots \; 2n+1 \#$$

Let us define

$$\delta = \frac{2\pi}{n}$$

Then the rectangular co-ordinates of the vertices on the top face (vertex numbers $i = 1, \ldots, 2n$) are:

$$x_i = R \cos i\delta$$
$$y_i = R \sin i\delta \quad (i = 1, \ldots, n; \text{ outer circle})$$
$$z_i = h$$

$$x_i = r \cos (i-n)\delta$$
$$y_i = r \sin (i-n)\delta \quad (i = n+1, \ldots, 2n; \text{ inner circle})$$
$$z_i = h$$

For the bottom face we have:

$$x_i = x_{i-2n}$$
$$y_i = y_{i-2n} \quad (i = 2n+1, \ldots, 4n)$$
$$z_i = 0$$

Here is the program for a hollow prism. By choosing n large enough we obtain a good approximation of a cylinder, as Fig. 6.3(b) shows.

```
/* HOLLOW_CYLINDER (preprocessor for HIDLINPIX)    */
#include <stdio.h>
#include <math.h>
main()
{ FILE *fp;
  int n, j, k, l, i, m;
  float r, R, pi, alpha, cosa, sina, x, y, z,
        delta, h, radius, hite;
```

```
printf("Give number n (n points on a circle):");
scanf("%d", &n);
printf("Give cylinder height:");
scanf("%f", &h);
printf("Give large radius R and small radius r:");
scanf("%f %f", &R, &r);
fp=fopen("cyl.dat", "w");
pi=4.0*atan(1.0); delta=2.0*pi/n;
fprintf(fp, "0.0 0.0 %7.2f\n", .5*h);
for (i=1; i<=n; i++)
{ alpha=i*delta; cosa=cos(alpha); sina=sin(alpha);
   for (l=0; l<2; l++) /* l=0: outer,  l=1: inner circle */
   { radius= (l==0 ? R : r);
      for (m=0; m<2; m++) /* m=0: top, m=1: bottom boundary */
      { k=i+l*n+m*2*n; hite= (m==0 ? h : 0);
         fprintf(fp, "%d %9.5f %9.5f %9.5f\n",
                 k, radius*cosa, radius*sina, hite);
      }
   }
}
fprintf(fp, "Faces:\n");
/* Top boundary face: */
for (i=1; i<=n; i++) fprintf(fp, "%d\n", i);
fprintf(fp, "%d\n", -2*n);
for (i=2*n-1; i>=n+1; i--) fprintf(fp, "%d\n", i);
fprintf(fp, "%d %d#\n", 2*n, -n);

/* Bottom boundary face: */
fprintf(fp, "%d %d\n", 3*n, -4*n);
for (i=3*n+1; i<=4*n; i++) fprintf(fp, "%d\n", i);
fprintf(fp, "%d\n", -3*n);
for (i=3*n-1; i>=2*n+2; i--) fprintf(fp, "%d\n", i);
fprintf(fp, "%d#\n", 2*n+1);

/* Vertical lines: */
for (i=1; i<=n; i++)
{ fprintf(fp, "%d %d %d %d#\n",
          j=i%n+1, i, i+2*n, j+2*n);
  fprintf(fp, "%d %d %d %d#\n",
          i+n, j+n, j+3*n, i+3*n);
}
fclose(fp);
}
```

6.3 BEAMS IN A SPIRAL

Our next example is a spiral as shown in Fig. 6.5. It is built from horizontal beams with length l, width w and height w. The bottom beam lies in the xy-plane, as shown in Fig. 6.6. Starting at the bottom, each next beam position is obtained by rotating the preceding beam about the z-axis through 90° and by incrementing its z-co-ordinates by a value w at the same time. We number the beams $0, 1, \ldots, n - 1$ from bottom to top. Beam i has vertex numbers $8i, 8i + 1, \ldots, 8i + 7$, assigned in a systematic way, such that the vertex numbers of beam 0 are as shown in Fig. 6.6. Every point (x', y', z') of beam $i + 1$ can be obtained by rotating the corresponding point (x, y, z) of beam i through 90° about the z-axis (and by setting $z' = z + w$), so we have

$$[x' \quad y'] = [x \quad y]\begin{bmatrix} \cos 90° & \sin 90° \\ -\sin 90° & \cos 90° \end{bmatrix}$$

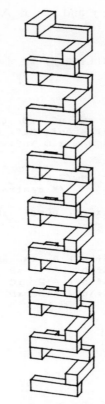

Fig. 6.5. Spiral of beams

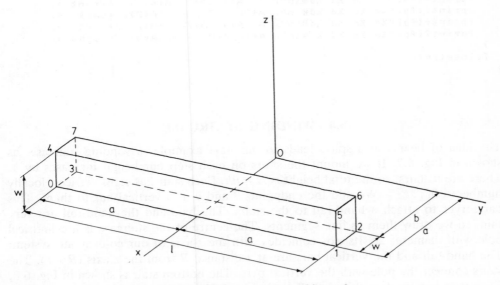

Fig. 6.6. Vertex numbers of beam 0

This can simply be written $x' = -y$ and $y' = x$. All this is used in the following program.

```
/* BEAMS (preprocessor for HIDLINPIX) */
#include <stdio.h>
main()
{ FILE *fp;
  int i, j, n, A;
  float l, w, xA, yA, xB, yB, xC, yC, xD, yD, a, b, aux, z;
  printf("How many beams?\n"); scanf("%d", &n);
  printf("The beam measures l x w x w.\nGive l and w: ");
  scanf("%f %f", &l, &w);
  fp=fopen("beams.dat", "w");
  fprintf(fp, "0.0 0.0 %f\n", n*w/2.0);
                                        /* central object point */
  a=0.5*l; b=a-w;
  xA=a; yA=-a;   xB=a; yB=a;   xC=b; yC=a;   xD=b; yD=-a;
  for (i=0; i<n; i++)
  { for (j=0; j<2; j++)
    { z=(i+j)*w; A=8*i+4*j;
        fprintf(fp, "%d %f %f %f\n", A,   xA, yA, z);
        fprintf(fp, "%d %f %f %f\n", A+1, xB, yB, z);
        fprintf(fp, "%d %f %f %f\n", A+2, xC, yC, z);
        fprintf(fp, "%d %f %f %f\n", A+3, xD, yD, z);
    }
    aux=xA;  xA=-yA;  yA=aux;
    aux=xB;  xB=-yB;  yB=aux;
    aux=xC;  xC=-yC;  yC=aux;
    aux=xD;  xD=-yD;  yD=aux;
  }
  fprintf(fp, "Faces:\n");
  for (i=0; i<n; i++)
  { A=8*i;
    fprintf(fp,"%d %d %d %d#\n", A,   A+3, A+2, A+1);  /*bottom*/
    fprintf(fp,"%d %d %d %d#\n", A+4, A+5, A+6, A+7);/*top    */
    fprintf(fp,"%d %d %d %d#\n", A,   A+1, A+5, A+4);  /*front */
    fprintf(fp,"%d %d %d %d#\n", A+3, A+7, A+6, A+2);/*back   */
    fprintf(fp,"%d %d %d %d#\n", A,   A+4, A+7, A+3);  /*left  */
    fprintf(fp,"%d %d %d %d#\n", A+1, A+2, A+6, A+5);/*right  */
  }
  fclose(fp);
}
```

6.4 WINDING STAIRCASE

The idea of beams in a spiral leads to our next example, a winding staircase, as shown in Fig. 6.7. If we mount the stairs on each step our height increases by h. There are n stairs, so the total height is $H = nh$. Each stair has eight vertices, locally numbered $0, \ldots, 7$. We add the endpoints 8 and 9 of a vertical bar to them. This bar serves to attach a hand-rail to the stairs. The bars and the hand-rail are very thin, so we draw them as line segments. The centre of the staircase is a cylindrical pole with diameter $2r$. Its axis coincides with the z-axis of our co-ordinate system. The hand-rail and the vertical bars are at a distance R from the z-axis ($R > r$). The stairs connect the pole with the vertical bars. The bottom stair is shown in Fig. 6.8. Each stair is a beam with length $R - r$, width $1.5h$ and height $0.2h$. Together the n

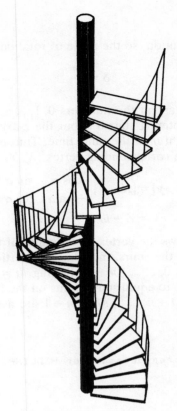

Fig. 6.7. Winding staircase

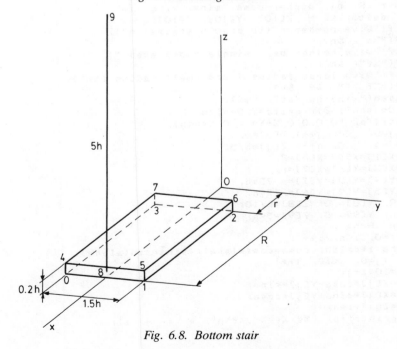

Fig. 6.8. Bottom stair

stairs constitute a full revolution, so the angle of rotation for a single step is

$$\delta = \frac{2\pi}{n}$$

From bottom to top we assign the numbers $0, 1, \ldots, n-1$ to the stairs. Stair i can then be obtained by rotating stair 0 about the z-axis through the angle $\alpha = i\delta$ and by raising it to the height ih at the same time. Thus each vertex (x, y, z) of stair i can be computed from the corresponding vertex (X, Y, Z) of stair 0 as follows:

$$[x \quad y] = [X \quad Y] \begin{bmatrix} \cos \alpha & \sin \alpha \\ -\sin \alpha & \cos \alpha \end{bmatrix}$$

$$z = Z + ih$$

In the program that follows the vertex co-ordinates of the bottom stair are stored in the arrays X, Y, Z. For the stairs, including the vertical bars and the hand-rail, we use the vertex numbers $0, \ldots, 10n - 1$. Setting $M = 10n$, we assign the next n numbers $M, \ldots, M + n - 1$ to equidistant points on the bottom circle of the central pole. Finally the integers $M + n, \ldots, M + 2n - 1$ are assigned similarly to the top boundary of the pole.

```
/* WINDING_STAIRCASE (preprocessor for HIDLINPIX)       */
#include <stdio.h>
#include <math.h>
main()
{ FILE *fp;
  int i, j, n, k, M;
  float r, R, pi, alpha, cosa, sina, x, y, z,
        delta, h, H, X[10], Y[10], Z[10];
  printf("Give number n (to draw n stairs)\n");
  scanf("%d", &n);
  printf("Give height of a single stair step ");
  scanf("%f", &h);
  printf("Give large radius R and small radius r\n");
  scanf("%f %f", &R, &r);
  fp=fopen("winding.dat", "w");
  pi=4.0*atan(1.0); delta=2.0*pi/n;
  fprintf(fp, "0.0 0.0 %f\n", 0.5*n*h);
  for (j=0; j<4; j++) Z[j]=0;
  for (j=4; j<8; j++) Z[j]=h/5;
  X[0]=X[1]=X[4]=X[5]=R;
  X[2]=X[3]=X[6]=X[7]=r;
  Y[0]=Y[4]=Y[3]=Y[7]=-.75*h;
  Y[1]=Y[5]=Y[2]=Y[6]=.75*h;
  X[8]=R; Y[8]=.0; Z[8]=h/10;
  X[9]=R; Y[9]=.0; Z[9]=5*h;
  M=10*n; H=n*h;
  for (i=0; i<n; i++)
  { alpha=i*delta; cosa=cos(alpha); sina=sin(alpha);
    for (j=0; j<10; j++)
    { k=10*i+j;
      x=X[j]*cosa-Y[j]*sina;
      y=X[j]*sina+Y[j]*cosa;
      z=Z[j]+i*h;
      fprintf(fp, "%d %f %f %f\n", k, x, y, z);
  }
```

```
    x=r*cosa; y=r*sina;
    fprintf(fp, "%d %f %f %f\n", M+i, x, y, 0.0);
    fprintf(fp, "%d %f %f %f\n", M+n+i, x, y, H+5*h);
 }
 fprintf(fp, "Faces:\n");
 for (i=0; i<n; i++)
 { k=10*i;
    fprintf(fp, "%d %d %d %d#\n", k,   k+1,  k+5,  k+4);
    fprintf(fp, "%d %d %d %d#\n", k+2, k+3,  k+7,  k+6);
    fprintf(fp, "%d %d %d %d#\n", k+1, k+2,  k+6,  k+5);
    fprintf(fp, "%d %d %d %d#\n", k+3, k+0,  k+4,  k+7);
    fprintf(fp, "%d %d %d %d#\n", k+2, k+1,  k+5,  k+6);
    fprintf(fp, "%d %d %d %d#\n", k+4, k+5,  k+6,  k+7);
    fprintf(fp, "%d %d %d %d#\n", k+1, k+0,  k+3,  k+2);
    fprintf(fp, "%d %d#\n", k+8, k+9);
    if (i<n-1) fprintf(fp, "%d %d#\n", k+9, k+19);
 }

 for (i=0; i<n; i++)
    fprintf(fp, "%d %d %d %d#\n", M+i, M+(i+1)%n,
                                M+n+(i+1)%n, M+n+i);
 for (i=M+n-1; i>=M; i--) fprintf(fp, " %d", i);
 fprintf(fp, "#\n");
 for (i=M+n; i<M+2*n; i++) fprintf(fp, " %d", i);
 fprintf(fp, "#\n");
 fclose(fp);
}
```

6.5 TORUS

In the winding staircase some dimensions (or rather proportions) were chosen
arbitrarily. We shall now discuss some examples where all vertices are computed
from a very limited amount of data. The first is a torus, as shown in Fig. 6.9.

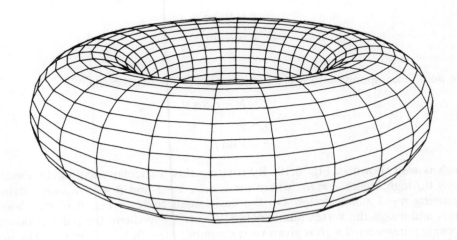

Fig. 6.9. Torus

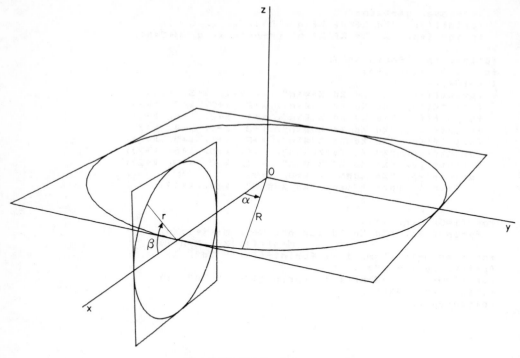

Fig. 6.10. Basic circles of torus

The input of the program will consist of three numbers, n, R, r $(R > r)$. In Fig. 6.10 the large horizontal circle is the centre circle of the torus; the radius of this circle is R. We choose n equidistant points on this circle as centres of small vertical circles with radius r. A parametric representation of the large circle is

$$x = R \cos \alpha$$
$$y = R \sin \alpha$$
$$z = 0$$

The point corresponding to $\alpha = 0$ is the centre of the small circle

$$x = R + r \cos \beta$$
$$y = 0$$
$$z = r \sin \beta$$

which is also shown in Fig. 6.10. By rotating this particular small circle about the z-axis through angles $\alpha = i\delta$, where $i = 1, \ldots, n - 1$ and $\delta = 2\pi/n$, we obtain the remaining $n - 1$ small circles. On the basic small circle in Fig. 6.10 we choose n points and assign the vertex numbers $0, 1, \ldots, n - 1$ to them: the point obtained by choosing parameter $\beta = j\delta$ is given vertex number j $(j = 0, 1, \ldots, n - 1)$. The next n vertices, numbered $n, n + 1, \ldots, 2n - 1$, lie on the neighbouring small circle, corresponding to $i = 1$, and so on. In general, we have the vertex numbers $i \cdot n + j$

$(i = 0, 1, \ldots, n-1, j = 0, 1, \ldots, n-1)$. A rotation through the angle $\alpha = i\delta$ about the z-axis is written

$$[x' \quad y'] = [x \quad y] \begin{bmatrix} \cos\alpha & \sin\alpha \\ -\sin\alpha & \cos\alpha \end{bmatrix}$$

In our situation the basic small circle lies in the xz-plane, so $y = 0$, which reduces this matrix product to

$$x' = x\cos\alpha$$
$$y' = x\sin\alpha$$

This result could also have been derived immediately from Fig. 6.10. The following program generates the file for the torus.

```
/* TORUS (preprocessor for HIDLINPIX)     */
#include <stdio.h>
#include <math.h>
main()
{ FILE *fp;
  int i, j, n;
  float r, R, pi, alpha, beta, cosa, sina,
        x, x1, y1, z1, delta;
  printf("Give number n (to draw an n x n torus)\n");
  scanf("%d", &n);
  printf("Give large radius R and small radius r\n");
  scanf("%f %f", &R, &r);
  fp=fopen("torus.dat", "w");
  pi=4.0*atan(1.0); delta=2.0*pi/n;
  fprintf(fp, "0.0 0.0 0.0\n"); /* central object point */
  for (i=0; i<n; i++)
  { alpha=i*delta; cosa=cos(alpha); sina=sin(alpha);
    for (j=0; j<n; j++)
    { beta=j*delta; x=R+r*cos(beta);          /* y  = 0 */
      x1=cosa*x; y1=sina*x; z1=r*sin(beta);   /* z1 = z */
      fprintf(fp, "%d %f %f %f\n", i*n+j, x1, y1, z1);
    }
  }
  fprintf(fp, "Faces:\n");
  for (i=0; i<n; i++)
  for (j=0; j<n; j++)
  { fprintf(fp, "%d %d %d %d#\n",
    i*n+j, (i+1)%n*n+j, (i+1)%n*n+(j+1)%n, i*n+(j+1)%n);
  }
  fclose(fp);
}
```

6.6 SEMI-SPHERE

Figure 6.11 shows the lower half of a sphere. We let the origin of the co-ordinate system coincide with the centre of the sphere. Since the whole picture will automatically be as large as the viewport, the absolute size is irrelevant, so we can choose a radius of unit length. Thus all points (x, y, z) of the semi-sphere satisfy:

$$\begin{cases} x^2 + y^2 + z^2 = 1 \\ -1 \leqslant z \leqslant 0 \end{cases}$$

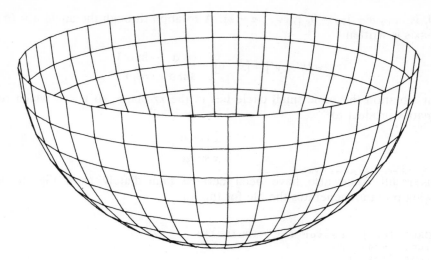

Fig. 6.11. Semi-sphere

Point $(0, 0, -1)$ is given vertex number 0. We shall divide a right-angle into n equal angles δ; this number n is the only number that our program will read. The relevant points on the semi-sphere with $x > 0$ and $y = 0$ are numbered $1, 2, \ldots, n$, counting from bottom to top. Their neighbours with $y > 0$ are numbered $n + 1, n + 2, \ldots, 2n$, and so on. This way of numbering is illustrated by the following table, where each (horizontal) row corresponds to points on a horizontal circle; similarly, each column corresponds to points on a quarter of a vertical circle:

$i \rightarrow$	0	1	2	$4n - 1$
j				
$\downarrow$				
n	n	$2n$	$3n$	$4n^2$
.	.	.	.	.
.	.	.	.	$\ldots$
.	.	.	.	.
2	2	$n + 2$	$2n + 2$	$(4n - 1)n + 2$
1	1	$n + 1$	$2n + 1$	$(4n - 1)n + 1$

The lowest layer of the semi-sphere consists of triangles, all having point 0 as a vertex. The remaining $n - 1$ layers consist of quadrangles ABCD; each quadrangle has two edges AB and DC that are horizontal and mutually parallel. Note that this semi-sphere differs fundamentally from the other examples that we have seen. It is not a solid object but a surface, which is visible from either side, depending on the viewpoint. Since each quadrangle has two faces, we specify both sequences ABCD and DCBA in the following program.

```
/* SEMI_SPHERE (preprocessor for HIDLINPIX)   */
#include <stdio.h>
#include <math.h>
main()
{ FILE *fp;
  int i, j, n, A, B, C, D, P, Q;
  float pi, alpha, beta, delta, cosa, sina, cosb, sinb;
  printf("Give number n\n"); scanf("%d", &n);
  fp=fopen("semi.dat", "w");
  pi=4.0*atan(1.0); delta=pi/(2*n); /* n * delta = pi/2 */
  fprintf(fp, "0.0 0.0 -0.5\n"); /* central object point */
  /* R = 1; sphere centre in O */
  fprintf(fp,"O  0.0  0.0  -1.0\n"); /* first point */
  for (i=0; i<4*n; i++)
  { alpha=i*delta; cosa=cos(alpha); sina=sin(alpha);
    for (j=1; j<=n; j++)
    { beta=j*delta; cosb=cos(beta); sinb=sin(beta);
      fprintf(fp, "%d %f %f %f\n",
                   n*i+j, sinb*cosa, sinb*sina, -cosb);
    }
  }
  fprintf(fp, "Faces:\n");
  for (i=0; i<4*n; i++)
  { P=i*n+1; Q=(i+1)%(4*n)*n+1;
    fprintf(fp,"%d %d %d#\n", O, P, Q);
    fprintf(fp,"%d %d %d#\n", O, Q, P);
    for (j=1; j<n; j++)
    { A=P+j-1; B=Q+j-1; C=Q+j; D=P+j;
      fprintf(fp, "%d %d %d %d#\n", A, B, C, D);
      fprintf(fp, "%d %d %d %d#\n", D, C, B, A);
    }
  }
  fclose(fp);
}
```

6.7 FUNCTIONS OF TWO VARIABLES

Program *HIDLINPIX* was designed to produce perspective drawings of solid objects. In two respects we have already seen that we can use it for other purposes as well. First, 'loose' line segments such as portions of co-ordinate axes can be drawn if we include their endpoints in the input file under the keyword 'Faces'. Second, in Section 6.6 we dealt with the surface of a semi-sphere as another mathematical abstraction. We shall now go a step further in using *HIDLINPIX* for purposes beyond our original goal.

We sometimes require a graphical representation of functions of two variables:

$$z = f(x, y) \tag{6.1}$$

We wish to specify a rectangular domain:

$$x_{min} \leqslant x \leqslant x_{max}$$

$$y_{min} \leqslant y \leqslant y_{max}$$

In principle, function f can be any continuous function of two variables. As an example we shall use the quadratic function

$$f(x, y) = ax + by + cxy + dx + ey + g \tag{6.2}$$

(We do not use the letter f as a coefficient because f is the function name.) The program will ask for the coefficients a, b, c, d, e, g and also for the integers N_x and N_y. These two integers are used to compute the following length and width of elementary rectangles:

$$\Delta x = \frac{x_{max} - x_{min}}{N_x}$$

$$\Delta y = \frac{y_{max} - y_{min}}{N_y}$$

The corners of these rectangles are the grid points (x, y) for which we actually compute $z = f(x, y)$. The three-dimensional points (x, y, z) thus obtained are connected by straight line segments parallel to either the xz- or the yz-planes. It is these line segments that will be drawn. Figure 6.12 shows the function

$$f(x, y) = 0.1x^2 - 0.4y^2$$

where we have chosen

$$-5 \leqslant x \leqslant 5, \qquad -2 \leqslant y \leqslant 2, \qquad N_x = 20, \qquad N_y = 8$$
$$\rho = 20, \qquad \theta = 50 \qquad \varphi = 80$$

We associate a pair of integers (i, j) with each grid point $(i = 0, \ldots, N_x; \ j = 0, \ldots, N_y)$. The point (x, y, z) of the surfaces that corresponds to grid point (i, j) is assigned vertex number $k = j \cdot (N_x + 1) + i + 1$. Then we have:

$$x = x_{min} + i \cdot \Delta x$$
$$y = y_{min} + j \cdot \Delta y$$
$$z = f(x, y)$$

The vertex numbering is illustrated in Fig. 6.13(a), where $N_x = 3$ and $N_y = 2$.

In Fig. 6.13(a) we view the surface from the positive z-axis. For example, points 1, 2, 5, 6 are points on the surface. Unfortunately, these four points will in general not lie in the same plane, so we cannot use them as vertices of a polygon. If we

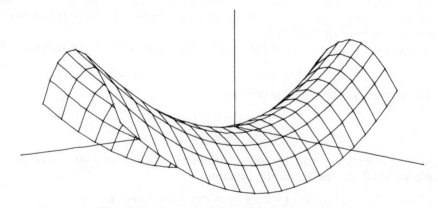

Fig. 6.12. A quadratic function of two variables

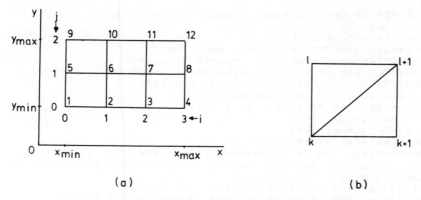

Fig. 6.13. (a) *Points on surface*; (b) *two triangles*

connect point 1 with point 6 we have two triangles that solve our problem. For the general case this is shown in Fig. 6.13(b), where $l = k + N_x + 1$. Though not co-planar, these two triangles can be used as the required polygons, provided that we prevent edge $(k, l + 1)$ from being drawn. Depending on our viewpoint, either side of the triangles can be visible, so under *Faces* we have to specify the triangles twice:

$$
\begin{array}{cccl}
k & -(l+1) & k+1\# & \text{(lower-right, clockwise)} \\
k+1 & l+1 & -k\# & \text{(lower-right, counter-clockwise)} \\
k & -(l+1) & l\# & \text{(upper-left, counter-clockwise)} \\
l & l+1 & -k\# & \text{(upper-left, clockwise)}
\end{array}
$$

The minus signs will prevent line segments $(k, l + 1)$ from being drawn.

Besides the function surface we shall also draw portions of the positive co-ordinate axes, as far as they are visible. Their lengths will be specified by the user. Finally, the program will also ask for some central z-value to be able to determine the 'central object point' required by *HIDLINPIX*. This is not particularly critical, so a rough estimation will do.

For quadratic functions of two variables the following program is quite general. For other functions $f(x, y)$ we can replace the function f at the bottom of the program and remove the program elements that have to do with the coefficients a, b, c, d, e, g.

```
/* FUNC: Perspective plot of a quadratic function */
#include <stdio.h>
float a, b, c, d, e, g;
main()
{ FILE *fp;
    int i, j, Nx, Ny, k, l;
    float xmin, xmax, ymin, ymax, hx, hy, x, y, f(),
          zc, xaxis, yaxis, zaxis;
    fp=fopen("FUNC.DAT", "w");
    printf("f(x, y) = a. x. x + b. y. y + c. x. y + d. x + e. y + g\n");
    printf("a, b, c, d, e, g:");
    scanf("%f %f %f %f %f %f", &a, &b, &c, &d, &e, &g);
    printf("xmin, xmax, ymin, ymax:");
```

```
    scanf("%f %f %f %f", &xmin, &xmax, &ymin, &ymax);
    printf("Nx, Ny:");
    scanf("%d %d", &Nx, &Ny);
    hx= (xmax-xmin)/Nx; hy= (ymax-ymin)/Ny;
    printf("Central z-value:"); scanf("%f", &zc);
    printf("Length of positive axes to be drawn (x, y, z):");
    scanf("%f %f %f", &xaxis, &yaxis, &zaxis);
    x= (xmin+xmax)/2; y= (ymin+ymax)/2;
    fprintf(fp, "%f %f %f\n", x, y, zc);
    for (i=0; i<=Nx; i++)
    for (j=0; j<=Ny; j++)
    { x=xmin+i*hx; y=ymin+j*hy;
      fprintf(fp, "%d %f %f %f\n", j*(Nx+1)+i+1, x, y, f(x,y));
    }
    k=(Nx+1)*(Ny+1);
    fprintf(fp, "%d %f %f %f\n", ++k, 0., 0., 0.);
    fprintf(fp, "%d %f %f %f\n", ++k, xaxis, 0., 0.);
    fprintf(fp, "%d %f %f %f\n", ++k, 0., yaxis, 0.);
    fprintf(fp, "%d %f %f %f\n", ++k, 0., 0., zaxis);
    fprintf(fp, "Faces:\n");
    for (i=0; i<Nx; i++)
    for (j=0; j<Ny; j++)
    { k=j*(Nx+1)+i+1; l=k+Nx+1;
      fprintf(fp, "%d %d %d#\n", k, -(l+1), k+1);
      fprintf(fp, "%d %d %d#\n", k+1, l+1, -k);
      fprintf(fp, "%d %d %d#\n", k, -(l+1), l);
      fprintf(fp, "%d %d %d#\n", l, l+1, -k);
    }
    k=(Nx+1)*(Ny+1);
    fprintf(fp, "%d   %d#\n", k+1, k+2);    /* x-axis */
    fprintf(fp, "%d   %d#\n", k+1, k+3);    /* y-axis */
    fprintf(fp, "%d   %d#\n", k+1, k+4);    /* z-axis */
    fclose(fp);
}

float f(x,y) float x,y;
{ return a*x*x+b*y*y+c*x*y+d*x+e*y+g;
}
```

EXERCISES

6.1 Write a pre-processor to draw several pyramids, some of which partly hide others, depending on the viewpoint.

6.2 Write a pre-processor to draw a full sphere.

6.3 Write a pre-processor to draw several semi-spheres, some of which partly hide others.

6.4 Choose one of the Exercises of Chapter 4 and write a pre-processor for it. We are now in a position to give a solution that is general in two respects:

– Hidden lines are eliminated by computation (in contrast to what we did in Chapter 4).

– The number n is variable. (In Exercise 5.2 we chose $n = 3$.)

6.5 Write a general rotation program in the sense of Exercise 3.2. The user will specify a vector **AB** and an angle α. The program is to read an input file for *HIDLINPIX* and to write another. In the latter file the co-ordinates will differ

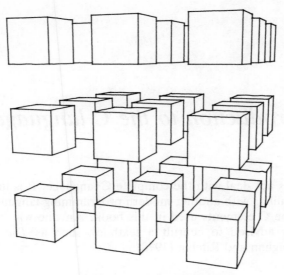

Fig. 6.14. A cube of cubes

from those in the former, according to the given rotation, so that a picture of
the rotated object will be the result.

6.6   Write a pre-processor to draw a great many cubes that are placed beside,
       behind and above each other (see Fig. 6.14).

APPENDIX

A brief introduction to the C language

This Appendix does not deal with the complete C language. It is intended for those readers who are familiar with another modern programming language and who want a brief survey of the C elements used in this book. Anyone who is going to use C actively is strongly advised to consult a textbook such as *The C Programming Language,* by Kernighan and Ritchie (1978).

A.1 BASIC DATA TYPES

Before we can use any variables we have to specify their types, or, in technical terms, we have to declare them, as, for example, in:

> *float xA, yA, p, q, r* = 5.0, *epsilon* = 1e − 6; *double dd;*
> *int i; short int si; long int li;*
> *char ch* = '*A*';

In their declarations, variables can be given initial values, as is done here for the variables *r, epsilon* and *ch*. We say that they are initialized. The numbers of bits that are used for the various data types depend on the hardware. On many machines, type *float* (single precision floating point) can effectively be replaced with type *double* (double precision floating point) to achieve greater precision. In the following we shall not always mention *double* explicitly, but regard it as a special case of *float*. Conversions from *float* to *double* and vice versa will never have effects different from what we expect. There is no 'Boolean' or 'logical' type in the C language. The integer value 0 acts as *false,* the value 1 (or any other non-zero value) as *true.*

A.2 SOME STATEMENTS

Consider the following fragment of a program:

> *if* $(x > = 0.5)$ $\{i = 10; j = 20;\}$ *else* $\{k = 30; l = 40;\}$
> *if* $(u < 3.0)$ $\{v = 1.8; w = 3.4;\}$
> *if* $(a < b)$ $m = n = 100;$

The meaning of these three if-statements will intuitively be clear. Notice that *if* is always followed by an expression between parentheses. An else-part is optional. Assignment statements such as

$$i = 10;$$

(and all other statements too) can be grouped together into a single compound statement by braces. Thus

$$\{i = 10; j = 20;\}$$

is a compound statement. We need them in if-statements if the execution of more than one statement has to be dependent on the condition. For example, if we had written

$$if \ (u < 3.0) \ v = 1.8; w = 3.4;$$

then

$$w = 3.4;$$

would have been executed anyhow, since the latter assignment statement has nothing to do with the condition $u < 3.0$. Braces are not used if only one statement is to depend on the condition, as the last of the three given if-statements shows. Here the multiple assignment statement

$$m = n = 10;$$

assigns the value 10 to both variables m and n.

A primitive loop can be set up by means of an if-statement and a goto-statement, as in

$$s = 0; \quad i = 1;$$
$$again: if \ (i <= n) \ \{s += i; i++; goto \ again;\}$$

Here $s += i$ and $i++$ are short-hand for $s = s + i$ and $i = i + 1$, respectively. These two lines are not meant as an example of well-structured programming. They merely serve to explain two new language concepts. The first is the while-statement, used in:

$$s = 0; \quad i = 1;$$
$$while \ (i <= n) \ \{s += i; i++;\}$$

This loop has the same effect as the previous one, so after i is incremented it is again compared with n and so on.

Another important construct is the for-statement, used in:

$$s = 0;$$
$$for \ (i = 1; i <= n; i++) \ s += i;$$

This piece of program has the same effect as the two previous ones, so in each of the three cases the following value is computed.

$$s = 1 + 2 + \ldots + n$$

Should n have the value 0 (or less than 0), then s will also be 0, since in all three cases the test for loop termination is executed at the beginning of the loop. This is not the case in the do-while-statement, appearing in:

$$i = 1; \quad s = 0;$$
$$do \ \{s += i; i++;\} \ while \ (i <= n);$$

Here the test for loop termination is executed at the end, as the notation suggests.

Thus the value $1 + 2 + \ldots + n$ is given to s only if n is positive. Should n be 0 (or less), then s obtains the value 1, in other words the inner part of this loop is performed at least once.

The statement

$$break;$$

can be used to terminate a while-statement, a for-statement or a do-while-statement unconditionally whenever this is necessary. Thus the effect of

$$i = 1;$$
$$while \ (i < = n) \ \{s + = i; \ if \ (s > MAX) \ goto \ ready; \ i + +;\}$$
$$ready:$$

is obtained without a goto-statement by writing

$$i = 1;$$
$$while \ (i < = n) \ \{s + = i; \ if \ (s > MAX) \ break; \ i + +;\}$$

or

$$for \ (i = 1; \ i < = n; \ i + +) \ \{s + = i; \ if \ (s > MAX) \ break;\}$$

To go immediately to the test for loop termination we can use the statement

$$continue;$$

For example, the while-statement

$$while \ (a < b) \ \{a + +; \ if \ (a < p) \ \{a + = 2; \ b + = 1;\}\}$$

can be replaced with

$$while \ (a < b) \ \{a + +; \ if \ (a > = p) \ continue; \ a + = 2; \ b + = 1;\}$$

A.3 OPERATORS AND EXPRESSIONS

Characters such as $+, -, <$ are used as operators to build expressions such as

$$a + b - c < d$$

If we write

$$x + y * z$$

we require the product $y * z$ to be added to x. Indeed, the multiplication operator $*$ has a higher priority than the adding operator $+$. Operators that have the same priority usually associate from left to right. For example, the expression

$$a - b + c - d$$

means

$$((a - b) + c) - d$$

There are also operators that associate from right to left. An example is the assignment operator $=$, since the assignment statement

$$i = j = k = 30;$$

has the same effect as

$$i = (j = (k = 30));$$

Note that = must not be used to test whether two values are equal; for the latter purpose we have the operator = =.

We shall now list all C operators; the meaning of some of them will be clear immediately, others will be discussed later. The operators are listed in order of decreasing priority, but those between a horizontal line and the next one have the same priority; they also associate in the same way.

( )	Function call		left-to-right
[ ]	Array element		
.	Structure member		
–>	Structure member using pointer		

(The following operators are said to be unary: they have only one operand. It should be noted that the characters –, &, * are also used as binary operators.)

!	Logical not	(see below)	RIGHT-TO-LEFT
~	One's complement		
–	Negative		
+ +	Increment		
– –	Decrement		
&	Address		
*	Indirection		
(type)	Cast	(see below)	
sizeof	Size in bytes		

*	Multiply		left-to-right
/	Divide		
%	Remainder		

+	Add		left-to-right
–	Subtract		

≪	Left shift	(see below)	left-to-right
≫	Right shift	(see below)	

<	Less than		left-to-right
< =	Less than or equal		
>	Greater than		
> =	Greater than or equal		

= =	Equal		left-to-right
! =	Not equal		

&	Bitwise and		left-to-right

∧	Bitwise exclusive or		left-to-right

	Bitwise or	(see below)	left-to-right
&&	Logical and	(see below)	left-to-right
||	Logical or	(see below)	left-to-right
?:	Conditional	(see below)	RIGHT-TO-LEFT
= *= /= %= += −= ≪= ≫= &= ∧= |=RIGHT-TO-LEFT Assignment			
,	Comma	(see below)	left-to-right

An expression may not only yield a value but also perform an action that changes the environment. The following line, for example, is an expression:

$$i = i + 1$$

This is an assignment expression, which increases i by 1. Less obviously, this expression also has a value, namely the new value of i. Hence it makes sense to write

$$j = 5*(i = i + 1) + 2;$$

which, incidentally, can be replaced with

$$j = 5*(+ + i) + 2;$$

Both $+ + i$ and $i + +$ have the effect that i is increased by one. However, they differ in the value they yield in the following sense.

$+ + i$ means: increment i and use its (new) value;
$i + +$ means: use the (old) value of i, then increment
this variable

Thus after the execution of

$$i = 5; \qquad j = (+ + i);$$
$$m = 5; \qquad n = (m + +);$$

we have $i = j = 6$, $m = 6$, $n = 5$.

An assignment expression and a semicolon (;), in that order, form an assignment statement. Thus

$$i = i + 1;$$

is not an expression but a statement (and so is $i + +;$). If several actions are required in a context where only an expression (and no statement) is allowed we can use the comma operator. Consider, for example, the loop

$$while \ (i + = j, \ j - -, \ k = i + 2*j, \ k > 0) \ j* = 2;$$

This works as follows:

$$again: \ i + = j; \ j - -; \ k = i + 2*j; \ if \ (k > 0) \ \{j* = 2; \ goto \ again;\}$$

(the meaning of $j* = 2$ is $j = j*2$, $j - = 3$ means $j = j - 3$, etc.)

The pair ?: forms another unconventional but useful operator. In the so-called conditional expression

$$cond \ ? \ expr1 : expr2$$

first the expression *cond*, denoting a condition, is evaluated. Then either *expr1* or *expr2* is evaluated, depending on whether the value of *cond* is non-zero or zero, respectively. Remember that *true* is 1 and *false* is 0 in the C language. Thus instead of

$$if \ (x > y) \ max = x; \ else \ max = y;$$

we can write

$$max = (x > y ? x : y);$$

It is important to distinguish between logical and bitwise operators. Logical operators are often used, as, for example, in

$$(x < 0 \ || \ y > 0 \&\& y < 1) \&\& !(z < 0)$$

which should be read as

$$((x < 0) \ or \ ((y > 0) \ and \ (y < 1))) \ and \ not \ (z < 0)$$

For the logical operators && and || it is guaranteed that the second operand is evaluated only if the first is not sufficient to decide what the final result will be. There is therefore no danger that

$$i > 0 \&\& j/i > k$$

should cause a division by zero.

The result of such a logical expression is always 0 or 1. On the other hand, if we use bitwise operators we think in bits, although we use integer variables, as, for example, in:

$$i = 5; \quad j = i \ll 2; \quad k = i | j;$$

Here the operations 'left shift' ($\ll$) and 'bitwise or' ($|$) are used. Written in binary, the values of i, j, k are now as follows.

$$i = 0 \ldots 000101 \quad (= \ 5)$$
$$j = 0 \ldots 010100 \quad (= 20)$$
$$k = 0 \ldots 010101 \quad (= 21)$$

The cast operation can be used to force type conversion. Thus the value of

$$(int)\ 3.95$$

is 3 of type integer.

If both i and j are of type integer, i/j is the truncated quotient. Thus 8/3 has the value 2, of type integer, even in a context where *float* is expected, as in $x = 8/3$, where x has type float. If at least one of the operands a and b has type *float*, the quotient a/b has type *float* and is not truncated. Float constants contain a period or the letter e (or E); integer constants have not. Thus:

1.5e3/50   has the value 30.0
7/4.0   has the value 1.75
7/4   has the value 1

The remainder operator % can be used for integer operands only:

37%5   has the value 2
37%5.0   is illegal
(int) 37.9%5 has the value 2

In the last example the cast operator (int) has priority over the remainder operator %.

If a float value is assigned to an integer, truncation will take place. Thus the statement

$$i = 3.9;$$

assigns the value 3 to the variable i. Even if variable x has type float, the following statement will assign the truncated value 7 (converted to float 7.0) to x:

$$x = 39/5;$$

A.4 LEXICAL TOPICS AND PROGRAM STRUCTURE

In most cases blank spaces and transitions to new lines have no effect on the meaning of the program. Sequences of the form

$$/* \ldots */$$

are ignored by the compiler; they are pieces of comment for the human reader.

Identifiers such as names of variables consist of letters and digits; the first character must be a letter. Here the underscore (_) is regarded as a letter. Taking this into account, and distinguishing capital and small letters, we count 53 distinct letters.

We can also use an identifier for a constant, as, for example, in

#define MAXIMUM 1000

After this 'pre-processor control line' we can use the identifier *MAXIMUM* as just another notation for 1000. It is the first example of a macro. A more interesting one is *MAX*, defined by

#define MAX(x, y) x > y ? x : y

This line has the effect that, throughout the rest of the program, any string

$$MAX\ (a,\ b)$$

is automatically replaced with:

$$a > b\ ?\ a : b$$

To obtain correct results in more complicated cases, it is wise to use parentheses, so we should actually define this macro as follows:

$$\#define\ MAX(x,\ y)\quad ((x) > (y)\ ?\ (x) : (y))$$

There are also control lines for file inclusion. We often use

$$\#include\ \langle stdio.h\rangle$$

The effect is the replacement of this line with the contents of file *stdio.h*, which is a 'header file for standard I/O'. If mathematical functions such as *cos* and *sin* are used, we need the control line

$$\#include\ \langle math.h\rangle$$

A program contains one or more *functions*. In the C language we have no sub-routines or procedures, just functions. Even the main program is a function, whose name is *main*. This is merely a matter of notation and terminology, since functions need not deliver a function value and can be invoked in exactly the same way as a procedure is called in other languages. This is shown in the following program, which reads the two-dimensional rectangular co-ordinates of two points P and Q and computes the distance between these two points.

```
/* This program computes the distance between
     two given points P and Q                          */

#include ⟨math.h⟩

main( )
{ float xP, yP, xQ, yQ;
    printf ("Give xP, yP, xQ, yQ:");
    scanf ("%f %f %f %f", &xP, &yP, &xQ, &yQ);
    print_distance (xP, yP, xQ, yQ);
}
print_distance (x1, y1, x2, y2) float x1, y1, x2, y2;
{ float delta_x, delta_y, distance;
    delta_x = x2 - x1; delta_y = y2 - y1;
    distance = sqrt (delta_x * delta_x + delta_y * delta_y);
    printf ("Distance: %f \n", distance);
}
```

The standard functions *scanf*, *printf* and *sqrt* will be discussed in Section A.9.

A.5 ARRAYS AND POINTERS

After the array declaration

the following five variables of type float are available:

$$a[0],\ a[1],\ a[2],\ a[3],\ a[4]$$

We can also write $a[i]$, where subscript i can be any integer expression whose value will be neither negative nor greater than 4. Subscripts always count from 0. Between the brackets in the array declaration, only integer constants may appear. Instead of numbers, we often use named constants, as in the following example, which also shows that arrays can have more than one subscript:

```
#define NROWS 10
#define NCOLUMNS 8
    . . .
    int table[NROWS][NCOLUMNS];
    . . .
    for (i = 0; i < NROWS; i++)
    for (j = 0; j < NCOLUMNS; j++)
    { . . .
        . . . table[i][j] . . .
    }
    . . .
```

If v is a variable, $\&v$ is the address of this variable, or, in technical terms, $\&v$ is a pointer to v. If p is a pointer pointing to some object, that object is denoted by the expression $*p$. The following program shows how pointer variables can be declared and used:

```
main ( )
{ int i, *p;
    i = 123; p = &i; *p = 789;
}
```

This is not exactly a practical program, but it shows that we can have access to a variable without using its name. Here p is a pointer to i, so $*p$ is equivalent to i. This means that the variable i will finally have the value 789 instead of 123.

The name of an array can be used as a pointer to its first element. Thus instead of $\&A[0]$ we can simply write A. If we have a pointer to an array element and we add 1 to it we obtain a pointer to the next element (no matter how many bytes each element occupies). More precisely, instead of $\&A[i]$, we can simply write $A + i$.

In their declarations arrays can be initialized if they have permanent memory space, that is, if they are either external or static. External variables are declared at the outermost level, that is, outside functions. The external arrays X and Y are initialized in the following program, which prints the value 5.75.

```
float X[4] = {6.0, 6.0, 5.9, 6.1},
      Y[4] = {−0.25, 0.25, 0.0, 0.0};

main( )
{ printf("%f \n", X[0] + Y[0]);
}
```

Static variables have the keyword *static* in their declarations. In the following program the arrays X and Y are internal to the function *main*, but they are static, which means that they, too, have permanent memory space and can therefore be initialized.

```
main( )
{ static float X[4] = {6.0, 6.0, 5.9, 6.1},
              Y[4] = {−0.25, 0.25, 0.0, 0.0};
  printf("%f\n", X[0] + Y[0]);
}
```

A.6 FUNCTIONS

In the C language a function may or may not have a function value. If it has, this value is delivered by means of a return-statement. As the name suggests, a return-statement causes an immediate return from the function. Thus the following two functions have the same effect.

$$int f(x) \ float \ x; \ \{if \ (x < 0) \ return \ -1; \ else \ return \ 1;\}$$
$$int f(x) \ float \ x; \ \{if \ (x < 0) \ return \ -1; \ return \ 1;\}$$

Incidentally, we can write a shorter version, using a conditional expression;

$$int f(x) \ float \ x; \ \{return \ x < 0? -1:1;\}$$

Note how we express that a function has an integer function value and a float argument. The functions above can be called in the usual way, as, for example, in

$$n = 3*f(X*Y) + f(X);$$

where X and Y are float variables. If an argument is declared float, we must not call the function with an integer argument. Thus if i is integer, $f(i)$ is not a correct call of our function f.

If a function does not deliver a function value it need not contain a return-statement. However, even then a return-statement can be used if we want an immediate return. We then simply omit the expression between *return* and the semicolon.

In most cases it is only the numerical values of arguments that matter. However, sometimes we want a function that assigns values to variables, which are accessible through the arguments. This can be accomplished by letting these arguments be pointers to variables. The following function interchanges the values of two integer variables:

```
interchange(p, q) int *p, *q;
{ int aux;
  aux = *p; *p = *q; *q = aux;
}
```

After the execution of

$$i = 1; j = 2; interchange(\&i, \&j);$$

the values of i and j are 2 and 1, respectively. Note that the arguments $\&i$ and $\&j$ are pointers, which are denoted by p and q within the function. Two elements $A[k]$ and $A[m]$ of integer array A can be interchanged by this function in the following way:

$$interchange(A + k, A + m);$$

Remember that $A + k$ is another notation for $\&A[k]$.

The above variable *aux* is said to have storage class *automatic*, which means that it has no permanent memory space. In contrast to this we have *static* and *external* variables, which are permanent. Automatic arrays cannot be initialized. A simple variable can always be initialized; if it is automatic, and declared in function F, it will have the initialization value each time F is entered. If it is static, however, it will have this value only the first time the function is entered. If the function is left and entered again later, a static variable will have its last value, whereas an automatic variable is undefined (if it is not initialized).

A.7 STRUCTURES

Several variables can be grouped together to a so-called structure. Suppose that we wish to store some information about points in two-dimensional space. For each point P this information consists of the rectangular co-ordinates x and y and a code to indicate whether the point lies inside a certain rectangle. Let us assume that there are the points P and Q. We can then declare

$$struct \; \{float \; x, y; \; int \; inside;\} \; P, Q;$$

We can now use the components of structures P and Q in the same way as other variables, as, for example, in

$$P \cdot x = 1.5; P \cdot y = 0.8; P \cdot inside = 1;$$
$$Q \cdot x = 2*P \cdot x;$$

Instead of the above declaration, we could have written either

$$struct \; point \; \{float \; x, y; \; int \; inside;\} \; P, Q;$$

or

$$struct \; point \; \{float \; x, y; \; int \; inside;\};$$
$$struct \; point \; P, Q;$$

These two versions have the advantage that the same structure type can be used later by simply writing *struct point* (as in the last declaration of P and Q), instead of *struct* $\{float \; x, y; \; int \; inside;\}$. Note that in this declaration we have to use the keyword *struct*.

Should we wish to get rid of this obligation then we can use another facility, which in general enables us to give a type a new name. Here we can write

$$typedef \; struct \; \{float \; x, y; \; int \; inside;\} \; POINT;$$

Now *POINT* is a new name for our structure type, and we can proceed with

$$POINT \; P, Q;$$

An array A of, say, 1000 points can be declared by

$$struct \ \{float \ x, \ y; \ int \ inside;\} \ A[1000];$$

or, if the name *point* is defined as above, by

$$struct \ point \ A[1000];$$

or, if *typedef* is used as above, by

$$POINT \ A[1000];$$

Now each array-element $A[i]$ is a structure consisting of the three components $A[i] \cdot x, \ A[i] \cdot y, \ A[i] \cdot inside$.

Structures are particularly useful in connection with dynamic memory allocation, since they can contain pointers to other structures. We can thus build lists, trees and so on. If S is a structure containing pointer field p then this pointer is $S \cdot p$ and the object pointed to is $*(S \cdot p)$. For the latter expression a special notation is available, namely

$$S -> p$$

where the two characters $-$ and $>$ suggest an arrow, and form a single operator.

A.8 DYNAMIC MEMORY ALLOCATION

Suppose that we have declared

$$char \ *p, \ *malloc(\ ), \ *realloc(\ );$$

Then p is a pointer to a character, and we can write

$$p = malloc(n);$$

where n is some positive integer expression, denoting a number of bytes. The effect is that, if possible, a consecutive piece of memory for n characters is allocated. If the required amount of memory is not available, p will have the value *NULL*. The latter is a special value for a pointer not pointing to a real object; it enables us to perform tests such as

$$if \ (p == NULL) \ \{ \ldots \ /* \ Insufficient \ memory \ */\}$$

The n bytes thus allocated are now available through pointer p. If, for example, the letter Q is to be placed in the ith position ($0 \le i \le n - 1$), we can write

$$*(p + i) = 'Q';$$

The memory space thus allocated can be released by

$$free(p);$$

Suppose that a block of n bytes, pointed to by p, turns out to be too small, and that it is to be extended, the desired new size being $N \ (>n)$. We can then write

$$p = realloc(p, N);$$

Now if p does not have the value *NULL* it will point to a block of N bytes; the first

n bytes of this block will have the same contents as those that p pointed to previously.

We can also allocate memory space for other data types. Let us assume that we want a sequence of k integers. Since the standard function *malloc* must know how many bytes we need we are interested in the number of bytes occupied by an integer. This number is expressed in a machine-independent way by

$$sizeof(int)$$

Another complication concerns the pointer types that we now need. We need a pointer to an integer instead of a pointer to a character. However, *malloc* will yield a pointer to a character. Type conversion can be achieved by means of a cast-operator. Therefore we write

$$int *p;$$
$$\dots$$
$$p = (int *)malloc(k * sizeof(int));$$

Here the cast-operator $(int *)$ says that the desired type is *pointer to int*. The jth integer $(j = 0, 1, \dots, k - 1)$ of the sequence is denoted by $*(p + j)$.

A.9   INPUT/OUTPUT

In the C language there are no special constructs for input and output (I/O). Instead, we use a number of standard functions along with a predefined structure type, called *FILE*. Details about these are included in our program in a very convenient way, namely by writing

$$\#include \ \langle stdio.h \rangle$$

The header file *stdio.h* contains a *typedef* declaration of the form

$$typedef \ struct \ \{\dots\} \ FILE;$$

Thus if we write

$$FILE *fp;$$

then variable fp has type *pointer to FILE,* and the compiler knows the details of the structure type *FILE.* Such a structure will actually be available through fp after a file is *opened* by

$$fp = fopen(file\text{-}name, mode);$$

where the arguments have the following meaning:

file-name	string containing the name of the file as it will appear in the directory;
mode	"r" or "w" for formatted input or output; system dependent for unformatted I/O.

The counterpart of *fopen* is *fclose*; *fopen* connects a file to our program and *fclose* disconnects it. The following program shows how we can write something to the file

EXAMPLE. If this file does not yet exist, it will be created.

```
#include ⟨stdio.h⟩
main( )
{ FILE *fp;
  int i;
  fp = fopen("EXAMPLE", "w");
  for (i = 1; i <= 4; i++)
      fprintf(fp, "i = %1d     i*i = %2d\n", i, i*i);
  fclose(fp);
}
```

After the execution of this program there will be the file *EXAMPLE* with the following contents:

$$
\begin{array}{ll}
i = 1 & i*i = \ \ 1 \\
i = 2 & i*i = \ \ 4 \\
i = 3 & i*i = \ \ 9 \\
i = 4 & i*i = 16
\end{array}
$$

Instead of *fprintf* we can use *printf* and omit the first argument, the output will then appear on the display of our workstation instead of on disk. The complete program would then read:

```
main( )
{ int i;
  for (i = 1; i <= 4; i++)
      printf("i = %1d     i*i = %2d\n", i, i*i);
}
```

In fact *printf*(...) is equivalent to *fprintf(stdout, ...)*, *stdout* being a file-pointer for standard output, declared in the header file *stdio.h*. The first argument of *printf* (the second argument of *fprintf*) is a format string containing pieces of text to appear literally in the output and *format items,* related to the remaining arguments. Here %1d and %2d are such format items; they specify that the values of i and $i*i$, are integer numbers, to be printed in one and two decimal positions, respectively. All other characters in the format string are printed literally. These characters include blank space and the newline-character, denoted by \n. In format items the letter d must be replaced with f if the associated data item is *float* instead of *integer*. Reading data is done similarly with

$$fscanf(fp, format\text{-}string, \ldots),$$

if the data are in a file on disk, or

$$scanf(format\text{-}string, \ldots),$$

if the data are to be typed in by the user. However, the remaining arguments must now be pointers, since *fscanf* and *scanf* must be able to assign values to variables through these arguments. For example, if a certain number must be given by the user, we can write.:

$$printf(\text{"}Give\ the\ number\text{:"}); scanf(\text{"}\%d\text{"}, \&number);$$

(Omission of & in &*number* is a notorious error.) If x has type *float* and xx has type *double*, we can read their values as follows:

$$scanf(\text{"}\%f\ \%lf\text{"}, \&x, \&xx)$$

The letter l in $\%lf$ is necessary because $\&xx$ has the type *pointer to double*.

The function value returned by *fscanf* is the number of elements that have been read, if any. It is zero or negative if none could be read. We can use this to test if the end of the file has been reached.

Analogous to *stdout* there is a standard file pointer *stdin*. The two calls $scanf(...)$ and $fscanf(stdin, ...)$ are equivalent.

A single character can be read and written in a more primitive way:

$$ch = getc(fp) \qquad \text{(input from disk)}$$
$$putc(ch, fp) \qquad \text{(output to disk)}$$
$$ch = getchar(\ ) \qquad \text{(input directly from user)}$$
$$putchar(ch) \qquad \text{(output directly to user)}$$

Here $getchar(\ )$ is equivalent to $getc(stdin)$ and $putchar(ch)$ is equivalent to $putc(ch, stdout)$.

If we test the last character that has been read, and we decide that it is to be read again next time, we can put it back into the input stream by:

$$ungetc(ch, fp)$$

The functions *printf, fprintf, scanf, fscanf* perform so-called *formatted* I/O, as the final letter f in their names indicates. Formatted files have a line structure, and numbers are represented as sequences of characters. For files on disk that are only to be written and read by our own programs it is more efficient to use *unformatted* I/O. This means that the internal and the external representation of the data are identical, so numbers will probably be written as binary words of a fixed length. For unformatted I/O we use

$$fread(bufptr, size, n, fp)$$
$$fwrite(bufptr, size, n, fp)$$

The arguments have the following types and meaning:

bufptr	*pointer to char*	A pointer to a block of memory (sometimes called a buffer)
size	*int*	Size in bytes of one data element
n	*int*	Number of data elements in buffer
fp	*pointer to FILE*	File-pointer

These two functions deliver an integer as their function value, which is the number of data elements that has been read or written. As with *fscanf*, we can use this value to test whether we are trying to read beyond the end of the file, since then the read attempt will fail and the function value of *fread* will be zero.

A.10 MATHEMATICAL STANDARD FUNCTIONS

Strictly speaking, the available set of predefined functions is not a part of the language. However, in practice it is convenient to have a list of such functions at hand. We have often used mathematical functions occurring in the following list, which shows function and argument types, along with a very brief indication about what the function computes.

```
double cos(x) double x;      /* cos x                       */
double sin(x) double x;      /* sin x                       */
double tan(x) double x;      /* tan x                       */
double log(x) double x;      /* ln x                        */
double sqrt(x) double x;     /* square root                 */
double floor(x) double x;    /* floor (4.9) = 4.0 etc.      */
double ceil(x) double x;     /* ceil (4.1) = 5.0 etc.       */
int abs(i) int i;            /* int absolute value          */
double fabs(x) double x;     /* double absolute value       */
double acos(x) double x;     /* arccos x                    */
double asin(x) double x;     /* arcsin x                    */
double atan(x) double x;     /* arctan x                    */
srand(seed) int seed;        /* initialize rand( )          */
int rand( )                  /* random number generator     */
long int time(p)             /* time in seconds, since      */
    long int *p;             /* 1 Jan. 1970 0.00h G.M.T.    */
```

Bibliography

Ammeraal, L. (1986). *C for Programmers*, Chichester: John Wiley & Sons.

Ammeraal, L. (1987). *Computer Graphics for the IBM PC*, Chichester: John Wiley & Sons.

Angell, I. O. (1981). *A Practical Introduction to Computer Graphics*, London: Macmillan.

Ayres, F. Jr (1967). Schaum's Outline Series, *Theory and Problems of Projective Geometry*, New York: McGraw-Hill.

Escher, M. C., *et al.* (1972). *The World of M. C. Escher*, New York: Harry N. Abrams.

Feuer, A., and N. Gehani (eds) (1984). *Comparing and Assessing Programming Languages Ada C Pascal*, Englewood Cliffs, NJ: Prentice-Hall.

Foley, J. D., and A. van Dam (1982). *Fundamentals of Interactive Computer Graphics*, Reading, Mass.: Addison-Wesley.

Forsythe, G. E., M. A. Malcolm and C. B. Moler (1977). *Computer Methods for Mathematical Computations*, Englewood Cliffs, NJ: Prentice-Hall.

Hopkins, E. J., and J. S. Hails (1953). *An Introduction to Plane Projective Geometry*, Oxford: The Clarendon Press.

Kernighan, B. W., and D. M. Ritchie (1978). *The C Programming Language*, Englewood Cliffs, NJ: Prentice-Hall.

Kreyszig, E. (1962). *Advanced Engineering Mathematics*, New York: John Wiley & Sons.

McGregor, J., and A. Watt (1984). *The Art of Microcomputer Graphics for the BBC Micro/Electron*, Reading, Mass.: Addison-Wesley.

Newman, M. N., and R. F. Sproull (1979). *Principles of Interactive Computer Graphics*, New York: McGraw-Hill.

Plum, T. (1983). *Learning to Program in C*, Englewood Cliffs, NJ: Prentice-Hall.

Index